Parenting with Heart and Soul

A Parent's Guide to Emotional Freedom with EFT

Kelly Burch

Parenting with Heart and Soul
A Parent's Guide to Emotional Freedom with EFT

Print: ISBN 978-1-908269-50-8
Digital: ISBN 978-1-908269-51-5
First Edition

Published by
DragonRising Publishing
The Starfields Network Ltd.
PO Box 3175
Eastbourne
BN21 9PG
United Kingdom
www.DragonRising.com

Printed and bound by CPI Group (UK) Ltd, Croydon, CR0 4YY

Parenting with Heart and Soul

A Parent's Guide to Emotional Freedom with EFT

Kelly Burch

Dedication

For my beautiful children, Charlotte and Jake, who teach me something new every day! Love you both with all the love energy I can!

For my husband, who is open to giving my parenting ideas a go, even when they are a little strange or don't immediately make sense. We make an awesome team. Love you. xo

For Silvia, who held my hand through the writing process and gave my aspects exactly what they were needing for this to come to fruition. Thank you, thank you.

Praise for *Parenting with Heart and Soul*

In her book, *Parenting with Heart and Soul*, Kelly Burch gives you a new way to relate with your Self and your beloved children: through the heart centre. This is such a refreshing perspective!

Having commenced my own energy-healing journey in 2001, when I studied Reiki (Usui Natural System of Healing), I thought I had experienced most realms of energy and healing. That was until a moment in 2013 when I discovered *Transformations with Kelly Burch and Energy EFT*. Kelly's YouTube video *Energy EFT for Terrible Mothers* helped me through a really difficult parenting moment and for this fact alone I am eternally grateful.

Modern society burdens parents with pressures to be perfect, but the reality is largely unattainable. Something's gotta give! A parent cannot do everything that is expected of them by these unrealistic expectations and still remain sane.

Most books about parenting seem to impose an unequal dynamic between the parent and child. The energy moving between each person resembles a power struggle rather than a joyous, loving, harmonious relationship. Fortunately, *Parenting with Heart and Soul* reveals an adaptable and relatable insight, taking you on a beautiful journey in which Kelly gently expresses her wisdom in a fresh, fun and lighthearted way. There are lots of practical ways to reduce stress, which is so important for modern parents, and your children can get involved in the process too.

After reading *Parenting with Heart and Soul*, the answer became clear and simple—come back to the heart centre, breathe and relax. Tap away the stress!

Happy reading!

—Merryn Padgett
Founder of Earth & Sea Creative
Reiki Master/Teacher (Usui System of Natural Healing)
Australian Reiki Connection Member
Diploma of Community Welfare
Diploma of Holistic Counselling Practice

Although I've been using and teaching tapping to my clients since 1999, Kelly's book on EFT and parenting is a refreshing read, full of fantastic tips on how to be more present with your kids with your whole energy. Since having my own children I've learnt what a wonderful gift tapping is for them and myself as a parent, and Kelly's book will help so many families navigate the wild ride of parenthood positively and lovingly. What a beautiful gift for these families to send what I call a 'tool for life' out into so many households! Well done Kelly!

Jacqui Manning aka The Friendly Psychologist
www.thefriendlypsychologist.com.au

In her book, *Parenting with Heart & Soul*, Kelly has mixed and distilled simple energy psychology exercises with easy and in-the-moment practical solutions for those confrontations *all* parents experience every day in the often challenging and confusing world of raising children.

Additional information details how parents can handle their own stresses before they interfere with the raising of their children. The more we as parents are equipped to deal with our own emotional issues, the easier it will be to be conscious parents and raise wonderful, happy and positively empowered children.

While parents will often make many inevitable mistakes, use of the techniques described by Kelly will help them to find new resources and to manage and create a harmonious and loving environment for themselves and their children.

Karl Dawson
EFT Founding Master, creator of Matrix Reimprinting, Hay House Author

By addressing the role of energy in raising children, Kelly is educating us all on a vital piece of the puzzle that is often missed as we strive to create a happy and healthy family. Kelly has blended her professional and personal approach to energy work beautifully in this book. Readers will identify with her and her family easily as she describes "real life" situations and guides you through techniques that you can begin to use immediately in your own home. I found Kelly's book to be extremely thought-provoking and empowering. I will be recommending EFT & Parenting to all my clients as I am confident they will all experience a happier and calmer household as a result of embracing Kelly's philosophies. Thank you Kelly for sharing your wisdom and experience in this fantastic book.

Kris Barrett
Nutrition & Health Coach
Author of *No Cows Today*

Parenting with Heart and Soul is a great, easy-to-follow and inspiring read. It takes the pressure off being the "perfect parent" and guides you in regulating your own moods and behaviours, enabling you to raise children with love and understanding instead of stress and confusion. You may find yourself identifying with ineffective parenting methods and eager to try out the practical tools and techniques that Kelly offers to manage and clear your own stress and the stress of your children.

Children and teens have a way directly or indirectly triggering our negative parenting behaviours. We, in turn, can have a negative influence our children's behaviour unless we can effectively learn to manage our own energy body stress. *Parenting with Heart and Soul* offers many *soul-utions* to managing our emotional responses as well as helping to teach our children to welcome, explore, honour and transform their own emotions. Emotions, after all, are energy. Instead of acting as if it's not there, clearing and transforming the emotional energy creates lasting positive changes not only for the child but the parent too.

Parenting with Heart and Soul covers managing sibling arguments, toilet training, sleepless nights, how to calm a child's fears and anxieties and more. Most importantly, it includes a variety of ways of managing our own stress. When we manage our own energy bodies and bring our system into balance and harmony, we teach our children that they are capable of doing the same.

I'm so pleased I found this joyful book. Any child on the receiving end of these gentle and understanding parenting techniques will feel acknowledged, accepted and loved even when they are experiencing and displaying difficult emotions. Well done Kelly Burch!

Form an orderly queue to get your hands on this book to help put the heart and soul back into your calm and loving family.

Wendy Fry
Emotional Health and Relationship Consultant - Author of *Find YOU, Find LOVE:
Get to the heart of love and relationship issues using EFT*

As an AMT EFT Trainer and mother of two very young children, I am writing this review from both perspectives.

Throughout the book I felt that Kelly weaved together the combination of insight and emotion, giving the reader not only an emotional journey through their own childhood but also a practical guide on how to help children with not only understanding stress but how to release it.

I especially enjoyed the personal stories because I can relate to bedtimes, mealtimes and most certainly the stress of getting children ready for school. I use EFT daily with myself but also with my children, when needed.

My children have been known to stop people in the street who might be upset to say, "Don't worry, my mummy does that tapping thing, she can help you," even, I might add, to people with animals.

This book not only resonates with me personally, but also professionally because I work with children in my practice. I see many children and teenagers expressing fear, anger and therefore stress. With this miraculous tool, we can help them to feel safe and calm and to create their own reality from a clearer vision.

The wishes at the end of the book are a fabulous way of sending the message to the universe of our intent as a collective vision. After all, our children are our next parents and our next generation.

I feel that this book is perfect for parents to be, parents/grandparents and professionals.

I highly recommend it.

Susan Kennard
AMT EFT Trainer
www.susankennard.co.uk

Illustrations by Charlotte Burch

Contents

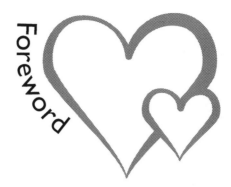

Foreword

Do you remember what it was like to be a child? How all things were immediate and overwhelming? Most of all, how often and how much we wanted for our parents to pay more attention to us, to just *listen* properly, so we could know that we were important and loved?

Has there ever been a child on this planet who has not sworn to themselves that they would do better when it became their turn to be a parent? And then we do—we "become parents".

A near death experience pales in comparison to the shock to the system that is! And when it happens, we are young and have hardly begun to figure out who we are ourselves, and then there are these others we are meant to raise.

The question has always been, "How?" How can we do better than our own parents? How can we keep our emotions in check, keep doing the right things even when we ourselves are distraught and tired and feel like we are drowning in chaos? How can we be better role models? How can we calm our children, get them to listen to us, obey us so we can keep them safe?

With so little practical or workable advice on the subject, we muddle through the best we can, but many of us feel we're letting our children down, that we're not the perfect parents these innocent souls truly deserve.

Finally, there is now a turning point.

An extraordinary and entirely revolutionary new idea has entered the human consciousness—we really do have an energy body, each one of us.

Children have one, too.

And when this energy body becomes disturbed, injured, stressed or too hungry, negative emotions come into being. Negative emotions— such as a child screaming louder than a fire siren "for no good reason", as the old folk would have it, because it has been fed, watered, and changed.

But that's not all a child needs. Far, far from it.

To take care of a child's energy body is of the utmost importance, not only to "grow a strong and healthy child", but to have a *happy* child. A child that connects, listens, interacts, plays happily, goes to sleep happily, learns *happily.*

A child that is a blessing and a gift to their parents.

Likewise, when parents learn to take care of their own energy bodies, they become better parents. More patient, more interactive, more in control, more willing and able to listen, respond, to play ... *happier* parents, in other words.

Happy children and happy parents together, creating happy families that are bonded strongly and provide the most important, amazing experiences for everyone. Love is set free and we are, quite literally, in a different world.

In this first book in the history of humanity on "the feeding and care of the human energy body for parents and children", Kelly Burch has shared with us her personal experiences in entering that world where energy is real, energy body stress is real, emotions—good and bad!—rule the day in every way, and the night as well.

Here, you find practical instructions and examples of how to apply modern energy techniques to revolutionise your experience as a parent and thereby create new futures for your children.

Please allow yourself to be very excited by this!

Also, please allow yourself a little time in applying these radical new principles and to find out for yourself just what happens when you do.

Energy is real. Our energy needs—unfulfilled, for the most part!—are very real and they drive all sorts of previously inexplicable behaviours. We all need more energy. We all need more love.

This book is the start of a new dawn, a new world.

And it is the book I wish my parents had read.

Silvia Hartmann

July 1st, 2014

Introduction

When my first baby arrived, *me who is a woman* was suddenly transformed into *me who is a mother*. I was thrust into this new title and role with no instructions or advice or information.

At times I felt like I was playing make-believe and that soon someone surely would show up and correct this error. As time went on it became clear that I was actually going to be trusted with the care and raising of this child.

So now what? How do I do this? How do I know if I'm doing it right or not? If my child is being a pain in the butt, does that mean I'm doing it wrong? If she or he sleeps poorly, throws a public tantrum, and refuses to eat the food I make, am I a bad mother?

Being an information-aholic, I absorbed a lot of information from books and websites relating to parenting. I found myself confused by contradicting pieces of information. What one person was recommending, another person insisted should *never* be done.

I was back to square one.

Some advice said I should trust my *mother's intuition*, but I was so challenged by the transition to motherhood (and the loss of some of the things that had previously made me *me*) that I found it difficult to tune into my own natural instincts and intuition.

So, many years and another beautiful child later, I am writing what I wish I could have read at the beginning of my motherhood experience! I'm writing about parenting with the support of the energy system and how it can make the process far simpler for you than it was for me.

I'm writing about techniques that relieve stress and confusion, that can allow access to intuition when it comes to parenting. Because of my professional experience working as an energy practitioner and trainer, I'm writing to share straightforward approaches and ideas of what not only works for me, but also gives predictable results.

I want every mum or dad, grandparent, teacher, or caregiver that is reading this, to be able to use the techniques described in this book to help them find their feet, their confidence and some peace when it comes to supporting a child. I want them to experience connection, compassion and love for the beautiful child in their care.

Introducing Energy

We all have an energy body. Although most people cannot see the energy body, it can have a significant impact on how we feel, respond and experience all life around us. In any situation where we have felt an emotion or a sensation in our body that had no physical cause (think of a churning tummy before a test or interview), our energy body was *speaking* to us and giving us a message.

Each person's energy body is unique to them, yet each one consists of energy channels, through which energy flows, and energy body parts, such as a heart centre, an energy mind and energy hands (Figure 1.1).

ENGAGING THE ENERGY BODY
Energy EFT

The Energy Emotional Freedom Technique (EFT) is one method with which to engage the energy body and give attention to any emotions or sensations that you wish to sort out. It involves gentle tapping on specific points that correspond to the body's energy channels in order to improve energy flow through the system. Any difficult emotions that you experience reveal that there is an energy blockage or disruption at some location in your body. You can use the tapping routines of EFT to give attention to that disruption and release it so you feel better. The usual result is that the difficult emotion is alleviated and your outlook is more positive.

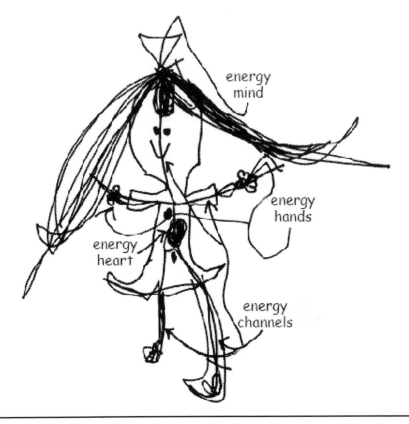

Figure 1.1 Energy Body diagram

Since its development in the 1990s by Gary Craig, EFT has been used on a variety of problems, such as phobias, with positive outcomes. EFT has also been the subject of many studies that have demonstrated it as an evidence-based technique that is highly effective in improving or eliminating symptoms of post-traumatic stress disorder (PTSD), depression and anxiety, to name but a few.

Diagnoses and professional treatments aside, EFT is a simple tool a person can use to support themselves emotionally when other techniques such as journalling, meditation, and Cognitive Behavioural Therapy (CBT) may not have been effective, especially when a person is under intense stress.

Heart & Soul Protocol

One soothing and supportive EFT technique is the *Heart & Soul Protocol*. With the help of breathing, gentle tapping and movement, you start to let go of any stress you are holding within your energy body (see the References for a link to a YouTube video I created demonstrating the basic Heart and Soul Protocol).

The Heart & Soul Protocol is easy to do and very effective for improving energy flow. Choose a Setup Statement (i.e., what you are aiming for with your tapping) such as, "I want to have free flowing energy!" Using the Setup Statement as a guideline, also choose a Reminder Statement as an abbreviated cue of what you are tapping for. For this example, I will use "Energy" as the Reminder Statement, but it will vary depending on what you are tapping for.

Begin by placing one hand over the other on the centre of your chest at the very place where you would point to yourself and say, "me". Take three deep breaths and say your Setup Statement. Now use the index (pointer) finger of your dominant hand to tap each point while you take a slow, deep breath and on the exhale say the Reminder Statement. The tapping steps (Figure 1.2) for the Heart & Soul Protocol are:

1. Gently tap on the centre top of your head, taking in a deep breath and on the exhale saying, "Energy!"

2. Gently tap in the centre of your forehead, taking in a deep breath and on the exhale saying, "Energy!"

3. Gently tap the inner point of one of your eyebrows, taking in a deep breath and on the exhale saying, "Energy!"

4. Gently tap the outer side of one of your eyes (on the bony part of the eye socket), taking in a deep breath and on the exhale saying, "Energy!"

5. Gently tap underneath one eye (again on the bony part of the eye socket), taking in a deep breath and on the exhale saying, "Energy!"

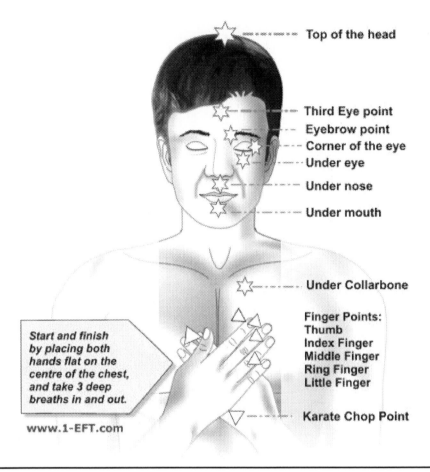

Top of the head

Third Eye point
Eyebrow point
Corner of the eye
Under eye

Under nose

Under mouth

Under Collarbone

Finger Points:
Thumb
Index Finger
Middle Finger
Ring Finger
Little Finger

Karate Chop Point

Start and finish by placing both hands flat on the centre of the chest, and take 3 deep breaths in and out.

www.1-EFT.com

Figure 1.2   Tapping Points for the Heart and Soul Protocol

6. Gently tap the area under the nose and above the top lip, taking in a deep breath and on the exhale saying, "Energy!"

7. Gently tap in the dip underneath the bottom lip and above the chin, taking in a deep breath and on the exhale saying, "Energy!"

8. Gently tap slightly under the collarbone on the knobby point where it meets the breast bone at a 90° angle, taking in a deep breath and on the exhale saying, "Energy!"

Move onto the finger points. Hold out your non-dominant hand as though you are going to shake hands with someone, thumb pointing upward. As you tap each finger, alternately move it slightly forward so you can tap on the top side of each finger, in line with the nail bed.

9. Gently tap the thumb, taking in a deep breath and on the exhale saying, "Energy!"

10. Gently tap the index finger, taking in a deep breath and on the exhale saying, "Energy!"

11. Gently tap the middle finger, taking in a deep breath and on the exhale saying, "Energy!"

12. Gently tap the ring finger, taking in a deep breath and on the exhale saying, "Energy!"

13. Gently tap the little finger, taking in a deep breath and on the exhale saying, "Energy!"

14. Move to the fleshy side of the hand that you would use to strike something with a karate chop. This area is commonly called the Karate Chop Point. Gently tap on this point, taking in a deep breath and on the exhale saying, "Energy!"

15. Return to the Heart Healing position, hands to the centre of the chest and take three deep breaths.

That is one round of the EFT Heart & Soul Protocol. It takes roughly 3 minutes to do a round of EFT and you can repeat it as many times as necessary on a particular topic to improve your energy flow and adjust how you feel.

If you are completing several rounds of tapping on any subject, the Setup Statement, and therefore the Reminder Statement, may change to reflect the changes in your energy. The Setup Statement may change from, "I want to have free flowing energy," on the first round to, "I want to have incredible energy," on the third or fourth round, and the Reminder Statement may change from, "Energy," to "Incredible Energy".

Important Notes: Throughout the Heart & Soul tapping, keep breathing deeply and encourage movement in any areas of your body that might feel stiff or tight, such as your shoulders or neck, and focus your attention only on what it is that you're tapping for.

The Setup Statement that you use is to draw your attention to a specific energy blockage that exists. It should be:

- **Meaningful to you.** It should *feel* right and let you feel the emotion or sensation as you think about it.

- **In your own words.** Your words are the perfect guide to your own energy system and rephrasing for grammar or censorship purposes may mean that attention is not being given fully to the energy disruption.

- **A single focus.** For best results you want to treat only one energy disruption at a time. Stick to one emotion or one specific sensation, word or short phrase. For example, don't tap for, "I am scared and lonely and unloved", because within the realm of *lonely* and *unloved* could be additional energy disruptions as well as the disruptions of being scared that were the initial focus. By all means do rounds of tapping for *scared* and then additional rounds for *lonely* and *unloved*, but keep to one subject at a time.

- **Resonant.** If you are tapping and feel nothing is happening, you've either shifted the energy blockage or you aren't giving full attention to it. Try tapping to affirm that you are safe in giving attention to things, with a setup of, "I am safe to give attention to this now", and a reminder such as "Safe". You could also focus on how it feels in your body as opposed to picking out *the right emotion*.

The SUE Scale

To measure how you feel beyond *good* or *bad*, use the Subjective Units of Experience Scale, or the SUE Scale (Figure 1.3). You can use the SUE scale as an indication of how you feel, from −10 (a strong negative emotion) to +10 (a strong positive emotion). Zero is neutral or no

Figure 1.3   The SUE Scale

emotion. You can also use it to check in with how you feel about something after you've done a few rounds of tapping.

Even after you are no longer feeling any negative emotion, keep improving your energy flow up the positive side of the SUE Scale. Go beyond feeling neutral so that you can feel even better, with improved energy flow and positive emotions and experiences.

Demonstration of Heart & Soul Protocol and SUE Scale

To demonstrate how to use the SUE scale and tapping together, I'll use an example problem of a woman named Sandra feeling worried about an upcoming event.

Sandra looks at the SUE scale and thinks, "When I think about this, how strong is the worry that I feel, from −10 to +10?" She runs her finger along the SUE scale and decides that −5 feels about right.

She creates a Setup Statement of, "I feel worried about an upcoming event", and taps for one round, using "Worried" as the shortcut to her Setup Statement. After one round of tapping, Sandra checks in with the SUE scale again. She finds that −3 describes how she feels and that her worry has eased somewhat.

She is still a little worried about the upcoming event, so she decides to complete a round of EFT tapping for, "A little worried". After tapping, she is feeling much lighter and finds that she is at 0 on the SUE scale and now feels unbothered about the upcoming event.

Even though Sandra is no longer worried, she thinks about the event and asks herself, "How do I *want* to feel about this?" She decides she would like to feel excited, so she adjusts her Setup Statement to be, "I want to feel excited!" and does another round of EFT tapping, using "Excited!" as the shortcut to her Setup Statement.

Sandra is now feeling really good after this round of tapping and feels tension leave her shoulders that she didn't notice was there. Smiling, she checks the SUE scale and finds she is drawn to +5.

She wants to feel even more excited, so she repeats another round of tapping for "Excited". With this round she is feeling tingles and warmth through her arms, legs and feet that she recognises as improved energy flow. She is practically jumping up and down thinking about this event. She now discovers she is really looking forward to it and is very keen to start preparatory activities. On the SUE scale she now finds herself at +10!

Energy Body Stress

Energy system disruptions happen when normal flows are blocked and are re-routed to other channels so that the system can continue to function. This means that some channels have limited energy flowing through them and some may be overloaded. This causes energy body stress. When you free up the blockages, you restore energy flow and reduce energy body stress.

Energy body stress can be understood as noise, or pollution of sorts, which confuses your energy system. If energy body stress is high enough, the flow of energy starts to grind to a halt. You no longer think, understand, connect, speak, express yourself, and/or move with as much clarity, coordination and ease as you did before. You start to show signs of tension, irritation, distraction, frustration, clumsiness, and confusion.

The graduated scale in the Energy Body Stress Table (Figure 1.4) shows that as the energy body stress worsens (or gets progressively closer to –10), the symptoms of that stress worsen, leaving people with reduced social skills and little interest in connecting with others. They become more irrational and worked up. If energy body stress is high enough, there will be symptoms of meltdown such as self-mutilation. Ultimately, at –10, they have such a high amount of energy body stress that the system cannot restore itself and it shuts down.

−10 So much stress damage that the system shuts down and does not restore itself (catatonia).

−9 Extremely high stress triggers a temporary shutdown of the totality (epileptic fit, panic attack followed by unconsciouness)

−8 Very high stress causing extremely severe disturbances (self mutilation, autism, blind rage, "going berserk," "madness")

−7 Very high stress causing extreme disturbances (extreme temper tantrums, self abuse, schizophrenic metaphors, "crazy ideas")

−6 High stress causing disturbances (temper tantrums, high-end addictions, illogical thinking, immediate gratification, unstable, highly egocentric)

−5 Full stress causing normal stress symptoms (irritability, can't concentrate, no control of thoughts and memories, communication failures, inability to enter into rapport with another, social, mental and physical malfunctioning)

−4 General stress (lapses in ability to control thoughts, emotions and behaviour, lack of long-term planning ability, overexcited, overly stubborn, closed minded, impaired communication skills

−3 Medium stress (talking, thinking and moving too fast, trying to do too much, putting in more effort than the situation requires, lack of empathy)

−2 Low stress (slight impairment in emotional control, not entirely "clear" on future goals and current situations, slight impairment in social skills)

−1 Low stress (occasional infrequent flashes of uninvited thoughts and negative internal representations)

0 No stress (calm, tranquil, peaceful, no action required, resting, relaxing)

+1 Very low energy flow (neutral, aware, occasional flashes of positive/ interesting internal representations and emotions)

+2 Low energy flow (vague sense of potential, hope, feeling like "waking up from a sleep")

+3 Medium energy flow (sense of wellness, feeling ok, smiling, beginning to move, enjoying the present)

+4 Improving energy flow (breathing deeply, increased body awareness, more movement, feeling good, starting to think about the future, able and willing to communicate freely)

+5 General energy flow (feeling wide awake, happy, ready for actions, wanting to take action, wanting to interact and communicate)

+6 Faster energy flow (feeling exciting physical sensations, more expansive thinking, feeling personally powerful, feeling excited, enjoying communication, high social awareness)

+7 Very fast energy flow (rethinking and reorganising concepts, expanded awareness, feeling powerful positive emotions, feeling alive, feeling love)

+8 High energy flow (increase in personal power, feeling delighted, making new decisions, very fast and logical thinking, high rapport and communication)

+9 Very high energy flow (delighted, unable to sit still, tingling all over, very excited, joyful, actively loving)

+10 Optimal energy flow (enlightenment experience, unconditional love)

Figure 1.4   The Energy Body Stress Table

Moving away from −10 toward 0, people gradually experience the absence of energy body stress. At 0 they feel calm and peaceful. As they move ever closer to +10, they go beyond this relaxed state and start to feel more hopeful and alert as their energy flow improves. They start to smile and laugh. They become more cooperative and clear, and have new ideas and understandings.

People can't help but move as the energy flow gets higher. They desire connections with others and experience insightful, intelligent and intuitive solutions to problems that baffled them before. They start to express themselves in *enlightened* ways. They are full of joy and happiness. They feel love; loving everything and everyone.

The interruption of stress and the enhancement of good energy flow are the potential for any normal human being on the planet.

You can assume that when someone smiles, laughs, moves fluidly and looks alive and bright, that their energy is flowing well. You can also assume that when someone is demonstrating antisocial, tense, irrational behaviours, they are experiencing high energy body stress.

If you are experiencing symptoms of energy body stress (take another look at the Energy Body Stress Table), the focus should then be on reducing that stress and increasing energy flow.

Observing Stress

Understanding what stress does to a person may make you mull over your own experiences when you lost your temper, said things you didn't mean, and behaved irrationally. It can also help you to understand what might have led to your child's tantrums and meltdowns.

I observed my children (and myself) over a period of time while considering these kinds of questions:

- Are there particular times of the day or the week when symptoms of energy body stress seem to be more prevalent?

- Are there common situations that easily lead to the increase of stress?

- Is it obvious that when we, as parents, do particular things, our child's stress levels reduce or increase?

I found that when my children's stress levels increased, they became more *naughty*, and ultimately lashed out, often after seeking my attention much more innocently early on.

I noticed that my son seemed more stressed and attention-seeking when he woke up in the morning when no one was available for play. I noticed that my daughter was more stressed at bedtime.

I noticed that the rush to get everyone ready for school was stressful for my kids (well, and me too). I noticed that when I was stressed, my children also tended to be stressed.

Most interestingly, I noticed that many of the typical parenting methods I was using were a source of stress for my kids.

Common Parenting Methods That Elevate Stress

When I understood that energy body stress contributes to how a person behaves and connects with others, I realised that the less stressed and more energised someone is, the better behaved they are. Once I understood this, it made no sense to do things that caused stress to the child and expected them to exhibit better behaviour. However, this non-sensical approach seems to be common to many parenting techniques.

Time Out

Consider the practice of putting a child in Time Out (Figure 1.5). Time Out is when a child is sent to a specific spot in the house where they are usually alone and have to sit or stand for a designated number of minutes before they can return to play. The idea is that the child will calm down, think about what they have done, and learn that it was not appropriate. They will learn not to repeat that behaviour. When the Time Out is up, the child can return to play, but if they repeat the same behaviour, they are again sent to Time Out.

Unfortunately, being put into Time Out can be a source of stress. If a child is experiencing difficult emotions they may be more in need of having support from a trusted adult or care-giver than in trying to struggle with these strong, difficult emotions on their own. Expecting a child, who has limited life experience, to improve how they feel or change their response to a situation without any support is putting a

Figure 1.5   A Typical Time Out

great deal of adult responsibility on the child. What experience is the child supposed to draw on to make that transformation possible?

I feel the act of sending a child to Time Out when they are misbehaving *does* send a clear message: "This behaviour is not acceptable and I don't want to see it." But once a parent understands how behaviour corresponds with the energy system, they know that the behaviour is more than just the behaviour itself and by using Time Out they are not necessarily treating the source(s) of stress that led to the emotional meltdown. Where does that leave the child? Telling them to stop is not helping them learn how to handle what they feel. Learning to do that is not an easy task for anyone, let alone a person who has been on the planet for perhaps less than 10 years. I believe that in order to comply with an adult's demands, the child has to bottle up the feelings that would otherwise show up outwardly.

Counting Down: 1, 2, 3

This method makes a statement that there will be a countdown to three and if the child hasn't done what is asked, there will be consequences. This method caused the biggest amount of stress in my kids whenever I used it to get them cooperate or get something done. The stress they had been feeling was not acknowledged in the experience and they were pushed to do what was asked in a very quick way. With this method there would always be shrieks of, "No!" and crying before they did comply.

In a sense, it *worked*, but it did not recognise what they were feeling. It taught them, in a nutshell, that I didn't care or want to know how they felt. I just wanted them to hurry up and do what I'd asked. While getting them ready for school on time (for example) was important, I *did* care what they felt.

Ignoring Bad Behaviour

Another common approach is for parents to ignore behaviour that they don't like and give praise to the behaviour they do like. This may be as straightforward as turning their back on a child, walking away from a tantrum, or not answering or responding when the child speaks in a particular way.

When it comes to ignoring a child's behaviour, the difficulty for them is that a situation or emotion may be quite overwhelming (especially if it corresponds with a state of high stress). Their parents' attention is actually what they *do* need in order for them to feel soothed, comforted, and reassured. They need to have someone there who will help them through their stress.

Depriving a child of attention may heighten their stress and their behaviour may worsen as a result. When a parent pretends they don't see the emotional/energy problem, it tells the child that when they are struggling, their mum or dad don't want to know about it. I'm personally not comfortable with that and would not choose it as a method because it does not show the child any respect.

Bribery/Reward/Taking Privileges Away

This method basically states, "If you do X, I will give you Y". It gives the child something that excites them or that they like, so they will do something they may not want to do. Now, I'm all for supporting someone's natural interests, but if you don't take the time to understand why a child doesn't want to do something, you are potentially telling a child they need to ignore a source of stress.

For example, if a child has difficulty with separation and cries when they have to go to kindergarten or school, telling them that if they don't cry they will get a chocolate does not acknowledge their stress. Their crying could be an expression of how they feel about being away from a care-giver and the safety of home. It is important for that to be heard and understood, even if it is inconvenient for the parent. Otherwise a child may feel the need to bury their feelings down in a place where it could fester and might establish a pattern when as an adult they turn to things like chocolate if they are upset and uncomfortable with expressing it.

If they are truly devastated, not only will they still feel devastated, but they will also miss out on something good *because* they are devastated. Those feelings are very real to them. It is a common source of stress to be alone, even for adults, and in this example the feelings of the child are disregarded.

Another example is toilet training: "If you poo in the toilet you get a sticker/lolly/toy". I have been in toilet-training hell myself, scrubbing poo out of underpants or even cutting my losses and throwing them in the bin. This stage of raising a child feels like it will never end and is unpleasant. No wonder parents are tempted to do anything they can to encourage their child to learn how to use the toilet.

The thing is, it can be quite stressful for a child to use a toilet. It is a gaping big hole and there are strange sensations in their body, unusual smells, and a big gushing and loud flush afterward that could possibly flush them out to sea! They can be so fearful that they withhold from pooing or weeing as long as is necessary until they are in the *safety* of a nappy. This isn't healthy for the body and may lead to urinary problems or constipation and further complications.

Receiving a sticker does not ease the very real fear of being washed away when the toilet flushes. Worse, not only does the fear remain, but the child misses out on something good. The child learns that feelings are a problem and, in addition, they possibly have let down their parent or themselves.

It is a difficult situation for a child to be in, especially when they are very likely trying to do their best. It's also difficult for the parent, wanting things to go smoothly and easily, and trying to find a method that best achieves this outcome. While I have certainly used rewards and bribery and refused access to particular privileges, I do not feel this method is respectful to the emotional/energy state that is likely to have caused the child's initial problem.

Smacking

I'm not a stranger to giving a smack on the bottom to get my child to listen or cooperate, but it is not an ideal strategy and certainly not one I would use as my discipline method of choice. The child's behaviour (lack of cooperation) is likely to be representing their energy body stress levels and then, when their parent gives them a smack, it is a shock and a discomfort. This only further exacerbates their stress levels.

In my experience it also doesn't necessarily work as a means of gaining cooperation because it further upsets the child and they become less communicative and responsive. And even if they are responsive, it is usually in fear of getting smacked again. As the person that is supposed to be the support and anchor in the child's life, that makes me feel quite uncomfortable.

I also noticed that the only times I would smack my children were when my stress levels were high. Smacking is not something I would do in a happy-go-lucky, excited and loved-up state. That tells me that *my* energy body stress makes a big difference, not only in how I am parenting my children, but also in how they are behaving. I believe that being aware of my own energy body state may be even more important than in how I discipline my children.

Parent Energy Body Stress

Not only are kids worse kids when they are stressed, parents are worse parents when they are stressed. When a person is stressed, they are usually irritable and overwhelmed with having to work harder than is needed to get things done. With the absence of stress and improved energy flow, they are happier, lighter, more insightful and engaged in a positive manner with the people around them.

Before I knew about the energy body, the onus was on my thoughts and willpower to make sure I was calm and patient and present. How could I do that when I was around –5 on the Energy Body Stress Table? At that level of stress I probably wouldn't feel up to playing delightful games with my kids. Every step forward took effort and discipline. That's exhausting and puts a lot of pressure on any parent in an experience that is already tiring and demanding.

It helps to take a step back and stop pushing yourself to control how you are thinking and feeling, and instead work with the energy body directly. When you make it your focus and priority to nourish your own energy systems, you gradually move up the Energy Body Stress Table in relation to where you normally *live* and your life improves as a result. You don't need to instantly be at a high energy flow forever onward, you just need to know that you can start bringing various elements of energy therapy into your day for gradual and steady improvement.

You have to remember that when you were a child your energy body and emotional states were not necessarily given supportive focus. You may have a lifetime of catching up to recognise how you feel and in learning to give attention to those feelings. You may be out of practice of doing this and find it is easier to stuff down how you feel or avoid it in the same ways that you were taught or learnt, by using food, shopping, alcohol, or video games. You need to learn to be patient with yourself and your experiences, the same as you can be with the experiences of your children.

Energy Tools for Parents

E ven when you have hectic days, you still tend to remember to brush your teeth at least once. You know it's beneficial for your general health as well as the health of your mouth, teeth and gums.

Supporting your energy system is also beneficial to your general health, as well as for the physical health of your body. Reducing stress has immeasurable positive flow-on effects to your well-being. So, just like brushing your teeth, I feel everyone should aim to do an energy treatment, morning and night. Done in the morning, it helps to start the day with increased energy flow and positive feelings, as opposed to what might instead feel like Groundhog Day—the same thing every day.

GOOD MORNING SHINE-UP

Your eyes open and if you're lucky there's no one beside you asking for food or drink or telling you they wet the bed.

If you do have a few moments to yourself, tune into your current mental and physical state. What are you thinking? What are you feeling? Notice any sensations within your body. Perhaps they are subtle or perhaps they are strong, like pain. What are you wishing for that would help you start the day feeling shiny and bright? Put it into a word or phrase.

Some examples could be "happiness", "relaxation", "beach holiday", "loving cuddle", "foot massage", "sexiness", "clarity", or "peacefulness".

This is your Shine-Up focus for the morning. Even if you picked several options, try to choose one focus at a time and really feel yourself *wanting* that, craving that, unashamedly!

If you are having trouble choosing a focus, ask yourself, "What would I ask a magic genie for if it appeared with one big wish available to me that would never result in harm to anyone else? What would I ask Santa for if he could give me anything at all, including moods and feelings?"

You're going to tap for that Shine-Up energy focus, whatever it is, and allow the energy of that Shine-Up to nourish you like fresh clean water rushing through pipes, clearing away debris as it goes. For this example I will use, "I want to feel amazing!" as the Shine-up intention and "Amazing!" as the Reminder phrase.

Begin by placing one hand over the other on the centre of your chest at the very place where you would point to yourself and say, "me". Take three deep breaths and say your Setup Statement. Now use the index (pointer) finger of your dominant hand to tap each point while you take a slow, deep breath and on the exhale say the Reminder Statement.

1. Gently tap on the centre top of your head, taking in a deep breath and on the exhale saying, "Amazing!"

2. Gently tap in the centre of your forehead, taking in a deep breath and on the exhale saying, "Amazing!"

3. Gently tap the inner point of one of your eyebrows, taking in a deep breath and on the exhale saying, "Amazing!"

4. Gently tap the outer side of one of your eyes, taking in a deep breath and on the exhale saying, "Amazing!" By now you should feel the energy start to move through you.

5. Gently tap underneath one eye, taking in a deep breath and on the exhale saying, "Amazing!"

6. Gently tap the area under the nose and above the top lip, taking in a deep breath and on the exhale saying, "Amazing!"

7. Gently tap the dip underneath the bottom lip and above the chin, taking in a deep breath and on the exhale saying, "Amazing!"

8. Gently tap slightly under the collarbone on the knobby point where it meets the breast bone at a 90° angle, taking in a deep breath and on the exhale saying, "Amazing!"

Move onto the finger points.

9. Gently tap on the top side of the thumb, taking in a deep breath and on the exhale saying, "Amazing!"

10. Gently tap on the top side of the index finger, taking in a deep breath and on the exhale saying, "Amazing!"

11. Gently tap on the top side of the middle finger, taking in a deep breath and on the exhale saying, "Amazing!"

12. Gently tap on the top side of the ring finger, taking in a deep breath and on the exhale saying, "Amazing!"

13. Gently tap on the top side of the little finger, taking in a deep breath and on the exhale saying, "Amazing!"

14. Gently tap on the Karate Chop Point, taking in a deep breath and on the exhale saying, "Amazing!"

15. Return to the Heart Healing position, hands to the centre of the chest and take three deep breaths.

Tune in to your body and notice how you're feeling. Check the SUE scale if that helps you to judge your emotion. If you are still on the negative side of the scale, you owe it to yourself to do at least two more rounds of tapping until you really do feel amazing!

Doing this Good Morning Shine-Up with inspirational or funky music that you love can also be a fantastic way to inspire a great energy state, as well as helping you to move your body while you tap. Movement is a great de-stressor and encourages energy flow at the same time. It will ease your physical body into the day.

This Good Morning Shine-Up is not going to eliminate the realities of what's going on in your life, but it is a great way to start the day as opposed to having an outlook of, "Here I go again. Same old..." Your intentions and expectations for your day can be quite powerful on your outlook. Many successful people talk about beginning the day with enthusiasm. Well, this is one simple way to shine up your outlook without having to convince yourself with a mind-over-matter discipline. Your energy body does the work as opposed to your brain.

GOOD NIGHT SPARKLE-UP WITH EFT

At the end of the day, when all the day's activities are done, I hope you will find a moment of peace for yourself when you can tune in and notice how you are feeling. Whatever happened during the day, you do not want to drag those things into your dreams (heaven forbid) and certainly not into the next day!

In the evening you can use EFT as a method to let go of the energy of the day's experiences and allow yourself to feel peaceful and relaxed, encouraging easy sleep and brighter mood.

Ask yourself: "What am I needing right now? What would help me to fall asleep easily and effortlessly? What will make me feel relaxed and happy?"

Your Good Night Sparkle-Up focus may encompass things like, "effortless sleep", "happiness", or "relaxation". It might also be things like, "goddess energy", "pampered queen", "nurtured", "starry sky", "freedom", "release", "let go", or "beautiful moonlight".

Your Good Night Sparkle-Up can be as magical as you want it to be. It should be something that makes you feel dreamy and beautiful. Something that really celebrates the night that has arrived, the moon and her magic, and the sparkling stars above.

What your energy systems need from one day to the next can be very different. This Good Night Sparkle-Up should never fall into the realms of autopilot and tapping for the same thing each time. Your energy body and mind should be the driver here, trusting in what intuitively comes up for your attention without analysis or conscious decision.

Using the same Heart & Soul Protocol detailed in the Good Morning Shine-Up, you can incorporate these additional options:

- You may want to spend longer in the Heart Healing position and soak up that beautiful heart energy.

- You may want to hold your intention silently, as a form of meditation.

- Instead of tapping, you may delicately hold or massage each point with a light touch.

- You may want to include candles, crystals, essential oils, peaceful music or luxurious fabrics as a ritual just for you.

- You may want to find a safe and comfortable place under the stars, moon and darkness and soak up the rich energy, complete with nature sounds such as crickets or leaves blowing in the breeze.

- If you are very tired, you may decide to do the Good Night Sparkle-Up while lying in bed before sleep. When you feel sleep calling you, move your hands into the Heart Healing position and breathe slow and steady.

A bonus of introducing this ritual to your evening is that it becomes a delight, something you look forward to. You don't need to seek some Me Time in television, the internet, wine, staying awake until the wee hours or scarfing down treats (though I admit I have done a Good Night Sparkle-Up with some red wine and chocolate at hand…sipping or nibbling along the way when it felt right). Instead, find some Me Time in this nourishing act of self-attention that supports you on many levels.

However you decide to do the Good Night Sparkle-Up, make it your own. Make it an experience that honours yourself and where you are.

ENERGY BODY DE-STRESS TAPPING TECHNIQUE

De-stressing is a go-to approach for reducing general stress levels as soon as you notice you are starting to get crabby. We're all different, but signs that might reveal you are under stress are annoyance at where your spouse has dropped their dirty socks, a need to send snarky text messages to said spouse, feeling that everything is too loud/smelly/ scratchy/uncomfy/icky/messy, feeling like the house is a bombsite even though no one has moved anything and when only the evening before it felt fine, sudden noises make you jump, stupid jokes seem stupid instead of hilariously silly, nothing is quite right, and you want to say "SHHHH" before realising a lot of the noise that is bothering you is in your own head with loops of churning thoughts.

You're not crazy, grumpy, or obsessive! You're just stressed, and you need to shift that stress to start to feel better.

I know firsthand that I am a better mum when I am relaxed and happy. I also know that when I am on edge and tense, my kids start to behave in kind. It is uncanny. They have become the proverbial *canary in the mine* that reveals my stress. If they are irritable, I start to look within and treat my own stress levels and wait for the storm to pass.

Free of stress, I am nicer and smile more. I respond to my kids with more patience and kindness. I have better ideas and tell jokes. We have more fun and the daily routine feels more fluid. Even if my family members are having their own difficulties, I can be more present to help them instead of frustrated at further stress or delay.

I highly recommend Energy EFT for de-stressing because it can be done no matter whether your stress level feels like –1 or –10 on the SUE scale. All you have to do is tap with the intention of reducing energy body stress and improving energy flow through your body (see the Energy Body Stress Table in chapter 1 as a reminder of symptoms of energy body stress).

Common words to use while tapping to de-stress are, "calm", "peace", "relax", "breathe", "flow", "centred", "soothed", and "serene". You can use any word that is soothing and that does not distract your focus from reducing your energy body stress.

Tapping to de-stress requires more steps than when tapping Heart & Soul Protocol.

1.   First, assess where you are on the SUE scale, from –10 to –1.

2.   Choose appropriate Setup and Reminder Statements for your de-stressing. You will be completing 2 rounds of tapping but with a slight change to help you more easily tackle your stress. Run through the tapping steps for the first round but instead

of going to the Heart Healing position at the end, return to the top of the head and start tapping again. The second round finishes normally, at the Heart Healing position and with three deep breaths. Encourage yourself with lots of deep breaths, movement and kindness as you go. You're doing wonderfully trying to de-stress!

3. Now, assess where you are on the SUE scale.

   a) If you are anywhere from –10 to –2, repeat another round to de-stress, tapping for whatever you feel would be soothing for you, or

   b) Determine if you are from –1 to +4 or +5 on the SUE scale. Tap a round for something that makes you feel happy and excited and energised. Energising words are as individual as you are but could include words such as, "sexy time", "freedom", "energy", "laughter", or "holiday!" If you get stuck, just go for straight up, "energy!"

4. Tune in again to the SUE scale to see where you are. If you are still below +7, go for at least one more round of something energising!

5. Enjoy the spoils of brighter and lighter energy.

It can be tough to find time alone to do tapping. If that is the case for you and you notice your stress levels are high, you can use one of the following options. I have used them myself:

1. Depending on their age, explain to your children you are feeling stressed and you need 15 minutes to calm down and feel better and you'll be back soon. If they follow you, either ask that they please wait until you are finished or that they join in with you.

2. If possible, hand over the parenting reins to someone else and explain to that person that you need to calm down. Tell them you know what you need to do to get calm and you'll be back soon. They may offer to talk to you about it, but assure

them that what you are going to do will be very helpful and, although you appreciate the offer, you would rather do what you have planned.

3. If your child is also upset and no one else is there to care for them, take them with you to a comfortable place, give them a book or just lie down near them and tap on yourself, saying your words out loud. They are likely to also benefit from hearing you breathe and feeling your energy shifts.

4. If you can't remove yourself from the situation, tap right where you are. If you are uncomfortable about this or are in public, such as on public transport or at a shopping centre, you can focus purely on the breathing and give subtle attention to the tapping points as though you are casually stroking your hair, brushing something from your face, or unconsciously touching your skin. You can also just try to visualise that you are tapping. This can be helpful, but the physical tapping and saying the Setup and Reminder Statements out loud are what will really anchor you to what you're feeling and be a more solid and grounding experience rather than an escape in your head. Another option is tapping only on your fingers, with two hands or one, which is convenient under a desk or table. It's also discreet and very easy to do one-handed finger tapping while walking somewhere, with the thumb tapping on the four other fingers of the same hand.

5. If your children are safe but arguing with each other and not listening to a word you're saying anyway, slip away to your room or even the bathroom and tap before re-joining them.

We are honestly giving ourselves and our families a gift with tapping. *It is not an act of selfishness or laziness*. It is one of the most important things we can do, not just in this moment in time, but for the future to come. Our experiences in the present are our memories in the future. The way we interact with our children is also helping to shape their future. While we have very little control over how they experience the world around them, we can acknowledge our role in building that world and ensure we do what we can to make it a better, happier place.

Ultimately, we can only do our best at any given moment. Even if we judge it as not being our *best*, it usually *is*, given where we are at the time and how we feel. If we know that we are feeling stressed, the best thing we can do is attend to it, not push it aside. It will grow and grow until we will be less in a position to support ourselves. You can probably guess how I know this...

CHILDREN HAVE EMOTIONS

Witnessing emotional expression in our child can be scary, like giant waves that have washed our kid away from us. Something has changed our sweet babe and transformed them into a monster, or a weeping sack of misery, or a jealous and competitive person instead of who they truly are.

Our children may show us anger so fiery and destructive that it scares us with how much power it has behind it. My usually sweet and light fairy of a daughter has described being so angry at times that she wanted to "STOMP on the whole world and crush it". Yikes.

We've seen children wail, whine and cry for days, seeking their comforters or the comfort of a parent, yet never seeming "filled up" by it. They are just endlessly miserable. We've seen our children experience wide-eyed fear so strong it made them run and hide or freeze.

Then there are the powerful forces of grief and loss, and the demonstrations of failure and disappointment when a child doesn't live up to their high expectations of themselves.

There is no denying that emotions can be powerful enough to affect minds and bodies. Regardless of age, emotions are deserving of attention and respect. What makes us want to stomp on the world when we are six may not mean much to a 36-year-old observing the world with their adult mindset, but that doesn't make it any less valid.

Emotions Are Only Energy Movements in the Energy Body

I know it's the heading of this section, but I'll say it again: "Emotions are only energy movements in the energy body."

We can know this because when we have an emotion we are also able to locate it in our body. If we ask a child, "When you think about this problem, where do you feel it in your body? Show me with your hands", they will be able to locate it. Try it yourself! Think of something that's troubling you and ask yourself where you feel it in your body. Without overthinking it, ask for your hands to show you. Once they do you will have found an associated energy blockage. This isn't taught, it simply is!

We often experience subtle sensations that are not strong enough to be labelled as an emotion, but that are definitely specific to an emotional reaction or trigger. Tiny prickles, circular wave motions, subtle tugging; all these are emotions too, but we just don't have names for them!

Embracing Emotions

Once we know that emotions and emotionally-associated sensations (without physical cause) are related to energy and understand how we can work with that, we can look on the expression of emotion in our child with new eyes. We do not have to fear any emotion in our children whatsoever. We can be more present with whatever it is they are feeling instead of trying to prevent it. Emotions in themselves are not a problem. There are no "good" or "bad" emotions. All emotions are valid and important.

The problem begins when emotions are stuck and impact negatively on a person's life. We can get angry and let it flash straight through us and be done with it. (I would not have believed that myself if it hadn't happened to me!) But we can also be angry, feel unable to release or express our anger and it remains lodged and is always present with us. Energetically, it is like a wound that is not healing itself naturally and may need intervention. Left indefinitely, this energetic wound may worsen and get more painful, inflicting some emotional pain, which is often seen as stress, tension, or difficulties in our everyday life.

Attention versus Ignoring or Distracting

Stuffing down emotion is not the answer. Neither is ignoring, denying, distracting or punishing it. Referring back to the stuck emotional wound analogy:

- We wouldn't tell a child to just forget about a bleeding wound on their knee.
- We wouldn't tell them if they stop thinking about it, it will go away.
- We wouldn't tell them to look at something shiny elsewhere to resolve their wound.
- We wouldn't yell at them to stop having a bleeding wound and to "get over it".
- We wouldn't give them a reward so that they will stop bleeding.

We know the best chance of healing and recovery from a physical wound would be with attention and care. It is the same for an emotional wound.

If a person is disciplined or criticised for feeling how they feel, they may bury that feeling deeper. It hasn't gone away, even if it is no longer being expressed. The unhealed energy wound is still in place because it has been denied the ability to complete its journey and be done and gone. Future experiences that knock on that wound are bound to trigger some emotional pain, even if the person does not remember exactly why. The wound is waiting for attention.

How to Handle Emotions

So, with all of the above in mind, the only way I understand to handle emotions as they arise in my children is *with as much presence, attention, openness, and connection as I can muster.*

I am their anchor, their solid ground, their unconditional support. Whatever the intensity of an emotion they feel, I am there, knowing that their emotions are *not* who they truly are, but an energetic expression that needs to happen.

For a parent to get to this point of understanding what a child needs may require a ton of self-support and care, but it is the ultimate goal and energetically provides the utmost support. You basically want your child to recognize that you see, feel, know and love all that there is about them, including when they are not sunny. I'm not always sunny and I hope that I am still loved! Our kids want that too.

And maybe, when they are on their own, they will be as present and loving with themselves as we were to them.

Their Emotions, Our Emotions

As parents, we need to be aware that our own internal representations of emotions come into play when we are with someone who is feeling or experiencing something that may have caused our own emotional wounds. I'm referring to emotional negative associations that we have learned through our lifetime. A common one is that anger is unsafe, but these associations are different for all of us.

Emotions in themselves are not contagious, but if you are sad on some level and you witness another person expressing deep sadness, you may also feel similar stirrings. Do not be scared of that and do not board up those windows to avoid letting out whatever is in there. It is something seeking your attention.

If sadness in your child makes you want to cry, cry along with them. Do not hide away the fact that emotions exist. Let your child know that emotions can be safely expressed. If their rage stirs up rage in you, stomp and punch pillows along with them. Done safely, this is a release for them and for you. It could also help them connect with you because they see how "Mummy gets it" and is on their side.

I have one major rule on emotions in my house: ***"You can feel however you feel, but you cannot hurt anyone else"***.

If the weight of your emotions (perhaps having waited your entire lifetime for expression) feels too much to handle, defer to a professional or another support person for their assistance in learning what it is your emotions are trying to tell you.

This is precisely the role you need to assume for your child. They *need* you to just be there, loving them, when they are feeling an emotion. They do not need you telling them to get over it or turning your back on them.

Explaining Emotions to Children

We can describe what emotions are to children in a way that reassures them that even strong or big emotions are still safe and normal and good. Here are some examples:

- Difficult emotions are stuck energy inside you. If you can let it move through you, you will feel more comfortable and happy.

- Difficult emotions are your body's way of telling you that it needs your help.

- You don't have to be scared of emotions because they can't hurt you. In fact there are emotions that feel great, like "fun!"

- Even really famous, beautiful, intelligent, and rich people have emotions. Having emotions doesn't make you bad. It makes you human.

- You don't have to hold onto either good or bad emotions. There is never any end to good feelings, so you don't have to store them up. Holding onto bad feelings just continues to make you feel bad, so you don't need to clutch them to you.

- Because emotions are made of energy, and everything has an energy, you can use anything to help you feel better. What makes you happy? What if you could have a big bucket of that kind of energy tipped on your head? Can you let that flow through you?

- Stuck emotions are like scrapes on your knee, but on your insides. Give them some love to heal them. It works even better than a band aid does.

Demonstrating teaches more effectively than words, so incorporate both the explanations as well as the presence with your child.

Emotions and Their True Energy

One day when I was sharing something about energy with my son, I realized that when I did energy work for him and his emotions and they were ones with which I had had some difficulty, I used a metaphor to describe what I had felt. This metaphor would always be a storm of some sort. Hailstorm, snow storm, thunderstorm, you name it. Later, I recognised that despite this storminess I felt when dealing with my emotions, the sun itself was always present, always there, behind the clouds.

Your beautiful child's true nature is like the sun, with blue skies and perhaps some fluffy white clouds. The storm is temporary and fleeting. Remember that when all you see is the storm and how it's affecting your life, the sun truly is always there (I speak from experience). The sun's beautiful power can be harnessed for good things in this world.

Heart Healing

This is a tool for those times when all hell has broken loose. You've probably felt stressed but haven't been able to attend to it for various reasons. Children going crazy, animals getting rowdy, phone ringing, someone at the door, mobile phone alerts pinging, worries going in a loop chasing their tails, pot on the stove boiling over, etc. Stress is at an all-time high and you feel that if you don't do something about it, you're going to explode and it won't be pretty!

When undergoing high stress, it's not a good time to analyse how you feel or use any cognitive methods that involve you consciously trying to control your thoughts and feelings. It is not only extremely difficult work, but it also adds to the *noise* of what you're experiencing and may increase the already high levels of stress. Approaches that involve analysis also tend to consider these stresses as a personal flaw; something that you have *chosen,* but if only you had more self-control, you wouldn't be feeling how you do.

When you consider the energy body and the energy body stress table, you can acknowledge that *increased stress makes everyone behave badly.* Your focus then is not on the behaviour, thoughts or feelings themselves, but on reducing your stress so you can be more yourself!

So…turn off the stove, do what you need to do to ensure that the children and animals are safe, ignore everything else for now and get thee to a quiet place alone.

Place your hands to the centre of your chest (in the Heart Healing position), and breathe deeply in and out. Repeat.

When your energy hands are on your heart centre and you are breathing deeply, you are not "just" breathing air in and out of your physical lungs, you are:

- recharging your energy "batteries",
- grounding and centring yourself,
- comforting and supporting yourself with attention to the heart centre, and
- reducing energy body stress.

You can continue this for as long as you need to in order to reduce your energy body stress and to feel human again.

What Do You Love?

One way to support yourself is to remember what it is that you love. Celebrate it and bring it in. Sadly, you may be so out of practice that you can't come up with anything. Your awareness of what excites you is so unused that it needs a bit of support. The resources from which you are working may be depleted. Your metaphorical cup is drained and things may feel quite flat and uninspiring.

In the fog of parenthood, especially in the early days (who am I kidding.... early *years*!), it can be easy to forget what used to light you up and help you feel alive. But if you can remember the past aspects of yourself who used to feel free and alive, you can ask yourself, "What do I love?"

You can use tapping to help yourself remember! Asking a question while tapping with Energy EFT can give you clarity and allow answers to come forward.

While in a calm state without distractions, tap at least 3 rounds for, "What do I love?" Allow your mind to experience whatever memories, thoughts, images, or sensations appear. Take your time with this and focus on supportive breath and movement as you go. You may feel a sense of grief or sadness relating to being out of touch with yourself.

This is okay. Keep going. It is only energy and we are working to be more in touch with what's in our heart of hearts! Use a notepad and make notes of what you love between each round of tapping (e.g., the beach, cafe with friends, chocolate). You should ideally finish up feeling excited remembering the things you love. Or learning about new loves! This may surprise you and not be what you expected.

With this knowledge, you have a ready-made list of things to integrate into your day. Each item on your list is something that you can enjoy by tapping for it! Being physically immersed in the things you love is amazing, but when you tap for the things you love, you can also become immersed in the experience of that energy and feel it across all of your senses.

For example, "beach" encompasses more than just a thought of sand and water. It can trigger within you the joy of past experiences and also the anticipation of future visits to the beach and fantasies of what you will do there. You may *feel* the sand between your toes, cool water curling around your ankles, the call of a seagull overhead, the laughter of friends and family, the excited cheekiness of splashing and playing, the restfulness of sitting on a towel and watching the world go by, the hush of the waves, the warmth of the sun, the smell of sunscreen, the sight of an orangey-pink sunset. You can tap for beach and recall or imagine all of these things.

When you use an energy technique like Energy EFT and tap for the things that you love, you are gifting yourself and your senses with (at the very least!) a taste of something nourishing for your souls, even if you cannot physically do these things!

When you have small children you may often be restricted physically as to what you can do or where you can go, but you have the luxury of the energy system still enjoying the spoils.

When you focus your attention on something wonderful and complete multiple rounds of tapping on our loves, you are likely to experience a mini-holiday feeling! This is a lovely state from which to go about your day! (Everything always seems much easier on holiday!)

So to sum up:

1. Think of what you love. If you can't pinpoint what that is, tap to help yourself remember.

2. Tap several rounds on this thing that you love, really immersing yourself in that feeling with all of your energy body and sensations switched on. You can also be as greedy as you want with these objects of love! You don't get ill from consuming endless amounts of chocolate *energy*.

3. Enjoy the mini-holiday feeling and filling up your cup with a hearty helping of those things that you love.

PROXY TAPPING

As well as tapping to support yourself, *you can tap on yourself to support others*. We are all connected energetically and like other distance energy work, such as Reiki or those moments when you think of someone and they call you out of the blue, this connection is real and tapping into it (ha!) is extremely powerful. We are not trying to control another person with proxy tapping, as everyone has free will to do what they choose, but to simply encourage movement in their energy system.

How to Proxy Tap

Instead of tapping for, "calm" for yourself, you might tap for, "Calm Johnny". Even though you are tapping on yourself, using all the tapping points and deep breathing and energy flow, you are actually tapping on behalf of Johnny's energy system.

We can be either very specific or quite general when tapping for someone else's energy system. For example:

- Jake's fear
- Charlotte's tummy ache
- Simon's unbelievable stubbornness
- Andrea's stress about her exam
- Jodie's sadness

In the process of proxy tapping for another, try to feel the energy of what is going on for them, as if it were your own difficulty, and encourage movement up the SUE scale.

One wonderful gift of working with energy and EFT tapping for another person is that any difficulty you feel within yourself in relation to that person is also attended to during the process. If you are tapping to help lessen Simon's stubbornness, you may not necessarily shift that trait for him but instead begin to see that Simon's stubbornness exists for a good reason. You may become more compassionate than you were able to be previously, having moved your own energy blockages in relation to Simon.

For this reason, it is wonderful to tap for your children or spouse and other people in your life. You can tap for something specific or something general (by using just their name, for example). By doing this you can help to keep your energetic relationships with them clear and be more compassionate and loving towards them.

To sum up:

1. Choose the person you're tapping for and what setup you will use.

2. Do a round of tapping for that person, with you as the proxy.

3. Check in on the SUE scale and get a feel for the level of the situation or experience.

4. Repeat until you feel bright, light and compassionate towards that person, or it feels *done*.

ASPECT TAPPING

Our personalities and energy are constantly evolving while still remaining *us*. Even though you are not the person today you were when you were three years old, you are still you. In the same way, your child is not the same child it was when it was a newborn but is still recognisably your child. This means that you, here and now, are unique, even though all those many versions of you that existed in the past or that will come into being in the future, are still aspects of you (Figure 2.1).

Lifeline Containing Infinite Aspects

Figure 2.1   The aspect with which you can work is the Now.

It is the same for every person.

You can't be two aspects at the same time, only sequentially. Consequently, one aspect may be a really good parent at 10 a.m. and then ten minutes later another aspect might have become very stressed and behave like a bad parent. As it is with you, so it is with your children.

This allows you to stop wondering whether you are a bad parent or a good parent, or if your children are wonderful and creative, or stubborn and uncontrollable.

Everyone has the capacity to become all these different things. Instead of saying, "I am a bad parent", it would be more accurate to say, "Last week, a former aspect of myself really lost the plot and started to scream like a lunatic".

When you think about it like that, it is much easier to understand what happened and why, and how future aspects might do things differently. You can then also understand how all aspects of yourself need love, help, support, and, I hope, be someone who can remind yourself that *under stress, any aspect can go crazy.*

FAMILY TAPPING

One way to lift the energy of the whole family, as well as encourage improved harmony in the household, is to tap together (Figure 2-2).

Figure 2.2   Family tapping lifts the energy of everyone involved.

There are many angles you can take with family tapping, but in my experience the best approach is to keep it light, quick, and enjoyable (as opposed to a drawn-out, family therapy kind of situation). Family tapping is great for those situations when there are lots of niggling little tensions, frequent arguments, or when people express (or demonstrate) that they feel unsupported or alone. It is an act of energetically improving the entire family unit for the benefit of all, individually as well as a whole.

I know first-hand that it may not be easy to get family members to tap along with you, but being very clear that it is quick, easy, and helpful, may make them feel better and convince them to join in. Happy family members also mean improved cooperation, potentially less fighting and more fun!

This should be tweaked for your own family's needs and the personalities of the members. Kids who are around 3 or 4 may not have the attention span to do more than one round of tapping, so that should be respected. It's not meant to be an arduous task and a drag. Older children may like further rounds and this is great. All family members (despite any initial grumbles) are likely to enjoy connecting with other members of the family.

How to Family Tap

1. Tell your family that you'd like to get all of them together and do five minutes of activity that will help them all feel great, as well as teach them something that will help them at other times if they choose to use it themselves.

2. Find a space that is comfortable and relatively clear, uncluttered and free of distractions. Decide if you'll sit or stand while tapping.

3. Ask your family members "What feeling do you think our family would benefit from having more of?" You or they might suggest things like, "fun", "playfulness", "love", "freedom", "happiness", or "harmony". Ask everyone to call out what they think, without judgement.

4. Whichever suggestion feels to be the most craved energy or feeling for the family energy system, tap one round on that. Say something like, "Okay, follow along with me. We're going to tap for happiness to bring in more happy energy for our family". Decide on words that feel the best, such as, "happy family", "happy home", or "more happiness for our family". If you sense it will help, feel free to play around with the wording a little as you proceed but the focus should remain on improving that particular energy for the family as a unit.

5. During the tapping session, keep it light, positive and encouraging. Say things like, "That's it", or "Very good!" If family members are flopping about or wriggling or laughing (instead of sitting still and quiet) it can be an indication of improved energy states and should be allowed to continue. In fact, if you notice still and tense family members, encourage them to relax and give their body some movement, such as rolling their shoulders.

6. Notice how the energy in the room feels during the tapping session, such as any shifts that you can see in the family members. Recognise that even if the single round of tapping doesn't completely transform everything (or it all goes pear shaped), it is still an experience that has evolved the energy of the family in some way. This is always a good thing! Congratulate everyone for joining in and ask for a repeat of the experience at a later time.

Remember, keep it light, easy, enjoyable, encouraging and relaxed. Follow your intuition and trust that the experience will be beneficial and offer something for everyone.

How to De-Stress a Child

An important skill in your parenting arsenal is to know how to reduce the energy body stress of your own child (Figure 2.3). There is, of course, tapping along with them, proxy tapping for them, or tapping for

Figure 2.3   An important skill is knowing how to destress a child.

something in front of them. Your child is not necessarily going to be willing to stop and tap with you every time they express a difficult emotion,
but there are other effective techniques that you can suggest when stress
starts to show up in their behaviour.

Breath. Encourage your child to take a deep breath, or even three.
It gets the energy moving and helps to relieve stress. It also stops the
child or shifts them down a gear and their stressed behaviour is less
likely to keep escalating. During breathing, hands to the centre of the
chest are optional but highly recommended.

Water. Water is a beneficial because it encourages energy movement as well as hydrating the child. I have seen water alone transform
a cranky child.

Movement. You rarely have to tell children to move their bodies, but if an upset child has been still for quite some time, encourage them to move around, stand, roll their shoulders, wriggle, or all of these. You could also encourage movement for them, such as by rubbing their back, stroking their hair, or stroking their arms.

Praise. Encouraging words from the heart are de-stressing and energising. If you can find a genuine way to praise a child, you can make a difference to their energy state.

Know What They Love. What does your child love? It could be something they do, play with, or experience. Whatever it might be, get to know more about it by hanging out with them. Do they have aspirations relating to this thing they love? What does it mean to them? Once you know what they love, you can talk about it or introduce elements of it at times when you recognise that your child's energy body is becoming stressed (irritation, anger, whining, etc.).

Intuition. You might get a flash of intuitive inspiration on something that would be helpful to your child. If you get a clear intuitive nod to give something a go (and it is safe), by all means follow it, even if it's not logically what your child might choose. This could be some form of game, some creative activity, a story that you are inspired to share with them, a particular place that you could take them, or information you could give them relating to something specific.

Space. A cluttered space can contribute to stress in children (and adults too!). Spaces that are clear make it easy to absorb the calm energy that is in them, especially for a stressed child. A small project could be to remove any confusing or disliked objects and any resulting clear spaces can used for a different type of toy. Storing things in cupboards or out of sight may also help.

Quiet. A lot of different noises from different things can add to stress that is already being experienced. When it comes to the energy body, sounds are information that is attempting to flow through us. If our energy body is already feeling bombarded and overwhelmed, noise is a further assault. Reducing noises, such as turning off unwatched TVs or music that can't be heard clearly, may help to calm a stressed child. If there is a lot of neighbourhood noise, closing windows and doors may help temporarily.

Light levels. Bright or flashing lights can also be a bombardment to the energy system. Moving to a dimly lit space may help to *reset* a child who is overwhelmed with stress. A child who is feeling relatively calm and happy may barely register bright lights, but if they become more and more stressed, the light levels can become too much for them.

It may be supportive to your child to establish some sort of rest or recovery space that they can seek out when they need it or at your suggestion. The space may encompass many of these de-stress suggestions such as a clear and uncluttered space that is quiet and subtly lit, may have something that they love, or may have a water bottle available and cushions or blankets to rest on. An older child might be interested in making a de-stress booklet or sign for themselves that could be a check list of sorts of things they could do to support themselves in moments when they are upset, such as, "Take 3 deep slow breaths in and out".

Other signs that are beneficial to know about that would cause energy body stress are:

1. If your child has not eaten or slept recently and is acting stressed, sleep, food and rest should be offered. It's possible that some physical or external factor is contributing to poor sleep. Either observe your child to see if you can determine what it might be or have a gentle discussion about their sleep habits.

2. If your child is behaving under the weather or not themselves, they may be unwell or experiencing some sort of physiological stress, such as an allergic reaction. Appropriate support for these kinds of problems should be sought, such as through a doctor, chiropractic practitioner, herbalist, homeopath, flower essence practitioner, or naturopath.

Part Three

Staying Calm When The Kids Are Driving You Nuts

I think you would be hard pressed to find a parent who has not once yelled at their child by the time they are school-aged. You have probably done it too. Yelling doesn't mean you are an awful ogre, it simply means you have reached a point when your levels of frustration and stress make you express yourself with force and volume (also see the next section relating to Communication on page 45).

I have some basic principles and action plans I follow when I encounter common parenting difficulties.

PROBLEM SOLVING FOR COMMON ISSUES

How to Avoid Yelling or Losing Patience

Basic Principles

The typical approaches to avoid yelling only target the yelling: control your voice volume and reward yourself when you achieve *x* consecutive days of not yelling. But the truth is, yelling is just a symptom and not the problem. Would you target the itching of the head or the head lice?

Chances are that you had already felt some form of stress long before you got to the point of yelling, even if it was very subtle. You probably don't yell or shout at your kids when you're in a good mood, but shouting comes easily when you wake up on the wrong side of the bed.

Figure 3.1   It's easy to shout when you're fired up!

Action Plan

1. De-stress at the very first *hint* of any kind of energy body stress. Take note of your own stress symptoms. For me, this is when I feel like sending critical text messages to my husband at work or when I feel like the house is filthy. Instead of sending those text messages or going on a decluttering rampage and throwing out possessions, I take it as a cue to de-stress. Once I do that, all is again well with the world.

    Determine your own stress symptoms and pay attention when these show up. Energy body stress can sneak up on you, especially in busy times when it is harder to tune into yourself.

2. If a lack of patience seems to persist even when energy body stress levels are reduced, encourage *more* patience on an energetic level by tapping for "patience". The pure and simple act of tapping for what you want encourages the energy of that desire to flow through you and clear away any energy blockages that might be preventing you from feeling it as your truth. Making statements while you tap that resonate with you can help also, such as, "I want to be more patient", or "I'm so patient!"

3. If there are repeated traits that your kids demonstrate, especially those that are actually harmless but still irritating, you can proxy tap for them. For example, "That clicking sound that Barry makes", or "Kerry's toothpaste smearing". During this process you are giving attention to the irritation as well as the things your kids are doing and their energy systems too. Proxy tapping is an extremely powerful tool for parents!

4. It is important for you to feel good in your daily life so that you have a big quota of free-flowing energy. This makes it harder for you to be annoyed by little things that your kids might do. Refer back to the What Do You Love? section in part 2 (page 31) and do more of these things you identified that help to fill your cup and have you feeling more in love with life.

Communication—Speech, Talking

Basic Principles

Communication is more than just words coming from a physical body. The energy system plays a big role in how you speak, or even whether you speak or not. When you are having a difficult time emotionally, when your energy system is stressed, you may:

-   Clam up, shut down, and/or find it hard to find the right words.

-   Refuse to speak lest you let loose with a flood of emotions.

Figure 3.2   When a child wants to speak, but can't, they may feel as though their mouth has a cage over it.

- Let fly with a torrent of generalisations that are unlikely to be true (e.g., "No one ever plays with me", "I never want to go to school ever again", or "I hate everyone!").

Speech is not just sounds omitted from between the lips, but an extension of what is going on inside of you. If you are stuck or scattered (which is the case in energy body stress), your speech may be filled with pauses, breaks and confusion, or jump from place to place without clear focus or direction.

A blockage in the energy system may exist around the mouth, throat or neck area and may also be contributing to speech difficulties. This can potentially arise from situations when it was difficult to speak or express your point or when you were unable to do so. My exploration of the energy system and autism found that the heart and the power of the energy system also play a role in speech, as though we need this heart fire to be powered up to a certain extent so that the *words in our heart* make it out to the world.

Action Plan

1. If you are the parent of a child who is not speaking, is stuttering, or is having difficulty speaking (such as might be found in a case of selective mutism), it is important to shift your focus from the speech issue and toward the child's energy state.

    Some questions that might be helpful:
    - Does this speech symptom arise only sometimes? In which circumstances is it worse?
    - Are there particular instances when this speech issue does not exist?
    - When did this begin and what else was going on for the child at the same time?

2. You can support your child by proxy tapping with EFT. You can use specifics gleaned from the above questions or be quite general. Beforehand, you should tune into yourself to feel if there is any stress that you are feeling about the issue and treat that with rounds of tapping to de-stress with such Reminder words as "relax", "calm", or "release stress".

    Example setups to use with Energy EFT proxy tapping could be:
    - Jane's mutism.
    - Charlotte won't speak.
    - Rudy's stutter.
    - Casper has stopped speaking.
    - Josh's speech.
    - Todd's missing words.

You should follow any intuitive or random thoughts that pop into your head while you are tapping on behalf of your child. These may seem random but could be significant and specific to the problem. You should tap for at least 3 or 4 rounds on this in one sitting, not to take the problem away, but to open-heartedly and open-mindedly give attention to what your child is experiencing. This pure attention can make a very big difference!

Proxy tapping can be extremely beneficial for you too, because in the process of tapping to help your child you are also simultaneously treating some of your own feelings about your child's issue.

3. You should not be afraid to bring in any energetic support that you need when you are tapping for how you feel about your child's situation, such as, "patience", "courage", "understanding", "acceptance", and "fearlessness".

These three steps can also be applied to other areas of difficulty with childhood development, such as listening and motor skills. Energy body stress can affect awareness, sensitivity (and being over-sensitive) and coordination. Any suspected physical issues (such as hearing problems or problems with gait) should be directed to a physician for attention.

Fears and Anxieties

Basic Principles

Children can be fearful of many things. My own children have been scared of art smocks, specific toys, wind, thunder, the toilet, food that looks different, life vests, being on their own, floaties, loud noises, darkness, dogs, nocturnal animals…should I go on?

It can be easy for us as parents to want our children to just move past the fears that show up in childhood, especially when it interrupts the flow of routine. It's also uncomfortable when a behaviour draws unwanted attention to us. It seems that no other child in history has had a problem with this fear and all the other parents are smiling smugly

Figure 3.3   Kids can be paralyzed when they feel bad things could happen.

with their cooperative and compliant child while our child is standing by the swimming pool refusing to get in. Loudly.

Fear is an energetic blockage relating to something. A perception of potential danger or a safeguard against a traumatic experience happening again. If a fear exists, it is for a valid reason even if it is because of an incorrect perception. A person with a phobia truly believes that something bad will happen in relation to that.

Action Plan

1. Based on the validity of a fear and the reality of an energetic blockage, step 1 has to be *respect the fear*. You don't have to like it, agree with it, or understand it, just respect that (for whatever reason) your child is scared of this thing.

   Respecting the fear means so much. It means:
   • Not forcing our child to ignore it and push past it by saying such things as, "You'll be all right, you're fine. Only babies are scared. Not you, you're a big boy".

- Not punishing them for having it or bribing them to ignore it by saying such thing as, "You won't be getting an ice cream like everyone else because you were naughty at swimming and refused to get in".

- Not expecting them to get over it just because we say so by saying something like, "There's nothing to be scared of, now hurry up and get in the pool".

We have to remember that we're talking about an energetic blockage. An energetic injury, so to speak. If this was a physical injury that was stopping your child from doing something, you would respect that and allow time for the injury to heal. You would not tell the child to ignore the pain. You would not punish them for being injured. You wouldn't expect the injury to heal just because you wanted it to hurry up and be healed.

It is incredibly important that everyone honour their own inner sources of information throughout their entire lifetime. When we respect that in ourselves, we are also teaching our children to respect it and value it, rather than ignore what might be their intuition, gut feelings, energy mind, etc.

2. It is important for parents to accept the child's fear as it is and use the support of EFT for however *they* are feeling about it. It's easy to imagine how difficult it will be for your child's whole lifetime when they are scared of something and feel stress about it. You want it to be taken care of. Acceptance doesn't mean that you're encouraging your child to be fearful, but are allowing things to be as they are for now, instead of resisting, forcing, stressing, or predicting.

It's the difference between, "Okay, so Tony is scared of dogs. What can I do to help him with that?" compared to, "This is ridiculous! Why can't he just pat it? It's just a dog. I don't get it!" When this happens, tap for *acceptance* or any other word or phrase that feels right to you, such as, "It is how it is", or "I accept Tony's fear".

3. Give calm attention to the fear. There are many ways this can be done respectfully when the fear is given some attention and the opportunity to change or shift gradually, without forcing or threatening.

    Proxy tap: Tap on yourself on behalf of the child's fear; e.g, "Simon's scared of ants". You may find this enlightens you as to why the fear exists.

    Pretend play: You can have toys or figurines that are scared of the same or similar thing that your child is. I did this when my son was scared of doing a poo on the toilet. I had Lego people really have to poo but were scared to. Other times (in different games) the Lego people did a poo without thinking twice.

    Play to where your child is and trust your instinct. In a very scared child, having the fearful toy (or fearful experience shown blatantly) could be too strong. On one occasion, I role-played putting a soft toy to bed, closing the door, and the soft toy crying and wanting mummy. My daughter was extremely upset about this. If it's not fun, it's not play anymore.

    Stress-free evolution: Ask yourself, "How can I take the stress out of this?" Come up with ideas that allow gradual exposure and improvement relating to the fear, and don't carry the object that is perceived as a threat to the child. These ideas are likely to come easier if you have already accepted the fear.

    For example, after my son had an incident at a swimming pool and felt unsafe, he refused to wear floaties on his arms at swimming lessons. Teachers tried and tried and he refused most passionately!

    I finally purchased a pair of floaties for the house. He avoided them, but I had them blown up and lying around. I wanted them to just be there so he could get used to the idea of them in a non-threatening way.

    I felt that the first step was for him to actually *touch* the floaties, but I couldn't force him to do this. So, I told everyone in the family that the floaties were special superhero handles that helped people to fly. I held them in my own hands and ran around the house as though I was flying. He joined in with flying around and found it funny. His sister wanted to do it too. Finally he *touched* them because he wanted to hold the floaties so he could use them like I had. YAY!

Next I put them in the bath so he could relate them to water. He still put them on his hands but seemed a little more wary. After some time for him to adjust to the floaties being with him in the water, we talked about how the superhero floaties worked best when they were around the arms and he put a forearm through one. (Cue mummy jumping for joy on the inside!)

Finally he had *both* floaties on and was flopping around in the bath tub. After that he wore them in his swimming class! Success!

We can trust that this gradual forward motion is a positive thing and that progress is being made when we are giving attention to the issue in some way. Positive and stress-free interactions in relation to the object of fear are informational experiences for the child and encourage softening and movement in the energetic blockage.

Handling a Kid That is Having a Meltdown

Basic Principles

When a child has *lost it* and is melting down, they've gone *way* past the point of calming down with the use of rationalisation and suggestions. They can't calm themselves down easily because they are too stressed, and at that point it is too much to ask of them anyway. They need you.

Any reprimands or disciplines at this point are (to me) unnecessary and ineffective and a bit cruel. Imagine yourself in a *crazy* state, feeling very out of control and fearful of what you might do. If at that point someone were to say, "Now if you stop that, I'll give you a chocolate", or "Stop it now or I'm leaving you on your own", imagine what

Figure 3.4   An overwhelming meltdown.

your reaction would be. It is unhelpful to the emotional state as well as unsupportive.

The child doesn't need to be disciplined or coerced at this moment, it needs to be supported in this unstable and shaky state of stress.

Action Plan

1. Keep calm and recognise that your child is really stressed right now. They might be hitting, kicking, shouting and demonstrating themselves in ways that make you fear for their future or wonder what is wrong with them. You may even wonder what you have done wrong in raising them. Stick to the energy of the situation: the child is a decent person but is stressed. You are a decent parent who is supporting this stressed child.

Your job is to be present and attentive. If you feel that you can't keep calm (and I get it, it's not easy), either tag team with your spouse or leave and take a 5 minute breather. You will be more effective in the long run than in staying and getting more stressed yourself. During your breather, do a single round of tapping to de-stress, with special emphasis on breath and the Heart Healing position. If your spouse has assumed the *present and attentive parent role*, support them by watching their stress levels and notice when they need a break.

2. Be present for the child. If they are willing, give them a hug, offer your lap or just sit near them. Give open and honest attention, without judgement or pressure.

    If they are trying to hurt you, hold their arm or leg firmly yet gently and state, "Do not hurt me". You are present, but not a punching bag. Depending on your comfort and their age or size, you can hold your child firmly in your arms if it helps them to settle down. Notice their response. If they get more stressed by this, it is not helpful and they should be released.

    During this process, a child may come closer but then push away, feeling stressed and wanting support yet also compelled to close off from people. Allow their natural expression of how they are feeling to happen.

3. Use soothing words and touch if they allow it. Say things like, "It's okay", "Deep breaths", or "I'm here". Apply gentle strokes to their back or arm if they are comfortable with this. Give loving attention to their heart centre, which can be from either the back of their body or on the chest. Just having a hand in that area, even hovering over it, can be soothing and relaxing.

4. If they have calmed down a little and are responsive to some questions, such as, "Do you want water?", it is time to encourage them toward thinking about things they love.

My son loves monster trucks, so I might ask him, "Which is your favourite monster truck?" I ask calmly and confidently with no urgent expectation of a response. Even if he can't answer, I know he has heard me. After a few moments, I might ask another question about monster trucks and bring in even more ideas associating with things he loves, such as, "What if there were monster trucks having a show at the Lego city arena and Pikachu was watching? Wow!" He might start to engage and respond with eye contact or smiling or words and this is *wonderful*.

The things that they love are energising to them and that is why they are worth mentioning. You are aiming to take them from the negative end of the SUE scale and that strong experience of energy body stress, to improved energy flow and feeling positive (at the positive end of the SUE scale).

You can usually recognise when they are in the neutral area of the SUE scale. They may act very tired with yawns, or even fall asleep, if they are tired enough.

5. When the meltdown is considered over, recharge *your* batteries with whatever you need: a hug from a spouse, a drink of water, tapping to de-stress, or deep breathing. You did an exceptional job supporting your child through that, even if they may not share their gratitude with you.

6. Think back and determine if there were any obvious contributing causes of stress for your child in this instance. What was happening prior? What had happened earlier in the day or the days before? Had the child eaten, rested, had water lately? Did the child receive attention recently? If the meltdowns happen frequently, there may be a pattern that shows up and it is worth noticing potential causes.

I know this wasn't all strictly using EFT, but our awareness of the child's energy body and encouraging movement of energy can be done with our attention and encouragement apart from the tapping skill of Energy EFT.

Handling the School Rush

Basic Principles

The process of getting organised and ready for school each day can prove difficult with some children! My free spirited and floaty butterfly of a daughter is one of them.

For this kind of child, sparks of imagination and dance happen spontaneously and are soaked up when they happen. But schools run to clocks and time, and the rush of getting several people clothed, fed, and prepped with everything they need each morning can be overwhelming and lead to very stressed mummies and daddies and irritated children!

Action Plan

Having been there and done that, I can tell you that yelling and forcing does not work! "Come on, hurry up, we'll be *late*!" just makes me and my children stressed, and causes my children to dig in their heels all the more.

1. De-stress. Tap to de-stress even before you're out of bed. Clear away that *here we go again* feeling. If this is a very long-standing and frustrating issue, tapping for something to signify positive change might help, such as, "anew!", "release the old", "evolution!" or "happy change!" Pick what resonates with you. The intention is to start the day with a positive outlook of your family having a wonderful morning together. Taking an extra 15 minutes to do this before your day starts will pay dividends.

2. Use your kids' unique personalities to support creative solutions that will get them ready on time and will improve their energy flow and de-stress them in the process.

   For examples:

   • Put on *getting dressed* music.

   • Have the toy cars watch how the child eats breakfast.

   • Call it superhero cereal and insist it needs to be eaten before the hero can save the day.

Figure 3.5   Getting some kids ready for school on time can be stressful for all involved.

- Sing while brushing their hair.
- If the child likes to lead, ask them to use a check list to decide what happens next.
- Make sure they have their super-fast boost shoes or magic enchanted secret spell shoes on.
- Ask the helpful child to manage the task of putting the lunch boxes where they need to go.
- Tell the game-loving child that they get 100 bonus points for putting shoes on quickly.

Cheer and encourage enthusiastically and genuinely when you can see that your children are loving what they are doing.

3. Use your *own* unique personality to support creative solutions for yourself too! (Hint: de-stressing makes it easier to come up with creative solutions.) If you get stuck, tap for, "I don't know how to (insert problem area here)" and see what inspiration strikes after a few rounds.

    Whether you are a morning or night person, planner or spontaneous, creative or structured, use it to your advantage in doing what you can to make the morning smoother. Whatever systems or solutions work for you and are not a source of stress, are the right ones.

    A lot of the flow of the morning comes down to how you, as a parent, feel and if you are feeling good, bright, ready and enthusiastic, this can flow on to your kids too and they become more cooperative as a result.

4. Give yourself a break if everything goes pear-shaped and you run late...if you forget the library book, spill the drink bottle, or your child's hair is a mess. Know that you're doing your best. Tap for it if you don't believe me.

Mealtimes/Picky Eating

Basic Principles

When it comes to energy, food can carry with it associations and experiences that are both negative and positive. So a carrot can be "deliciously sweet" to one person and "that thing that chokes me" to another.

A stressed state can result in high sensitivity to different smells, textures and tastes. I found this out when I thought I had a naturally heightened sense of smell. It turns out, this was only the case when I was stressed. When I notice that everything starts to smell strongly, I take it as an energy body stress symptom and tap!

Meals can be torture, a battle between parents trying to get kids to eat new food and kids refusing...loudly. I honestly have felt that I hate dinnertime in particular. Why dinnertime? Because it is the one meal when we are more likely to be sitting together and focused on the food, ensuring that the children have eaten well and have full tummies before

Figure 3.6   Ah, the dinnertime battle...

they go to bed. Being at the end of the day, the kids are typically tired and fussy and it becomes a source of stress. Dinner can be the perfect recipe for difficulty!

Action Plan

We need to take out all possibilities of stress from food, meals, and sitting together as a family. *All* of them.

Whichever of these examples stand out as a source of stress for you (and your family) should be tapped for:

- Kids not eating right and getting sick.

- Kids refusing beautifully home-cooked meal.

- Kids not sitting on their bottoms.

- Kids getting food everywhere.

- Kids not eating enough and being awake all night.

- Kids eating too much and getting a tummy ache.
- Kids playing with their food.
- Kids poking each other instead of eating.
- The noise of the meal time.
- The loud refusals.
- The timing of the meal.
- The time ticking away and feeling like the kids will go to bed hours late because they're eating so slowly or not at all.
- The frustration in not being able to satisfy everyone with one meal.
- Not knowing a solution.

If you experience stress for all of these examples, tap for all of them with words such as "happy dinnertime", or "enjoyable meal". Watch them climb the SUE scale and feel energised with how you *want* to feel instead.

Aside from clearing the sources of stress listed above, there are these points to consider:

1. This is possibly the one time of the day that everyone is together. Think of ways you could make it more enjoyable and effortless.

2. Good food should be presented, even if it's not eaten, and allowed to be tasted without pressure. Encourage sniffing, licking, chewing, or even spitting it out. It's all part of the spectrum of trying food.

3. Understand that different or unusual foods may be a source of stress, so a calm and positive environment is going to be more conducive to trying new things.

   Ensure that you too are trying different tastes and textures and expressing your genuine enjoyment of the meal. You are showing that food is interesting and an adventure and nothing scary or intimidating. It's also more than just going through the motions of eating—grinding teeth, mashing it and swallowing it. You are showing your children how to eat on many levels for that moment and into their future.

If there's a food that is particularly troublesome, proxy tap for that food and your child, such as, "Simon hates peas". We have our own tastes but it cannot hurt to give attention to it energetically.

4. Have some ground rules that you insist on, but for the rest, let go. Elbows on the table, eating with fingers and making cars out of salad ingredients won't hurt anyone.

5. Separate from dinnertime, ask the family what goals they may have during the time spent eating dinner together. Have a Family Tapping session when the agreed on goals are encouraged with everyone tapping for them.

Siblings Fighting—Not Sharing, Bossing Each Other Around

Basic Principles

Stressed people fight, refuse to share and require control. Relaxed and happy people are more able to negotiate calmly, recognise that there is more than enough for all, and be more comfortable to go with the flow.

There might be age-specific reasons that are contributing to children refusing to share and *play nice*, but stress is one of the most significant factors and the one we should focus on. How a child acts towards others should not be treated as an isolated event to be stopped, but a message relating to something bothering them when it comes to their world around them and their belief in what they will have and receive. If a child is constantly stating, "This is *mine* and you can't have it!" they may feel that on some level they are inequitably having to give up on the things they want.

Action Plan

1. The stress of not knowing how to confidently handle a clash can result in extreme reactions: screeching, wailing, hitting,

Figure 3.7   Siblings fighting can seem like a wild storm.

running off, exaggerations like, "She never...", or "I always...", usually followed by "It's not fair!"

When your children clash, the first step is to always reduce your own frustration with the squabbling so you can be the clear and calm anchor for them to lean on. Take yourself away from the fray if you need to and do a round or two of Energy EFT on "peace", "calm", or "relax" before coming in as the light and bright mediator. Your job is not to tell the kids what to do or solve their problems but to hear them out and give them attention. This becomes much easier without personal stress.

2. If a particular child seems hell-bent on annoying their sibling, this indicates some level of energy body stress and that is what needs to be targeted. You can do a bit of first-aid and treat the typical sources of energy body stress by:

   • Taking the child away for one-on-one time.

   • Giving a snack.

- Giving water.

- Encouraging a rest and relaxation session by reading a book together, or something of a similar nature.

- Giving positive feedback and praise whenever possible.

- Tap with them or for them (for example, tap on yourself while in the child's company and saying something like, "Happy Sarah").

- Giving attention to their heart centre by placing a hand on that spot and encouraging them to breathe deeply and relax.

3. If you feel that the child is pushing a sibling's buttons because of a specific issue, take time later to proxy tap for that (for example, "Jodie's fear of never getting what she wants", or "Nigel's freak-outs when he loses"). This proxy tapping may help shed light on what is going on for the child as well as to encourage shifting energy for the child.

4. Statements such as, "Leave her alone!" or separating the children at the first hint of a fight may deprive the children of the opportunity to learn how to sort out difficulties.

    If you stay calm along with them you can help to move things forward if they get stuck by making suggestions, such as, "Do you think we could work out how both of you could play with this?" or "Let's take turns with ideas on what to do next?" This encourages them to learn a skill with a maturity far beyond their years. Conflict becomes something to move through together without any need for panicking, aggression, or avoidance.

    In the process of discussions, you can work to keep the energy body stress to a minimum by asking questions about the things that the children like while giving positive feedback by saying things such as, "That's a great suggestion!"

or "I can see you're trying really hard to come up with ways to share".

5. Ensure that the most compliant child is not pressured to be the one who always gives in or agrees to play elsewhere or with other toys as a way of resolving the issue. This is not a resolution and teaches the compliant child that their needs are less important and should be put aside for the sake of peace.

Sleep

Basic Principles

Sleep is the act of slowing down and surrendering to tiredness and allowing yourself to rest. When you are occupied with thoughts (good or bad) or worries, this is not a simple task. It's also difficult when you are feeling tense or stressed. Often the tension you feel is not obvious and it may seem that you just can't sleep for no good reason. An inability to sleep often indicates that there is a something that needs to be released before you can settle down and allow sleep to happen.

Children's sources of stress are different from adult's sources. Children are not lying awake thinking about bills and health, but they may still be kept awake thinking about things that confuse or upset them, such as why things happened (like unusual sounds, leaves falling off trees, toys doing unexpected things) or uncertainty about their safety. They may also have tension (energy body stress) surrounding the actual process or environment of sleep: their room, the comfort or discomfort of their bed or cot, the transition from being with parents to being on their own, or their fear that scary dreams may recur.

There could also be other relatively simple contributors, such as needing something to eat or drink, needing to go to the toilet, being too hot or too cold, just not tired enough for sleep, or that they have a pain or ache. The comfort given by a parent's presence may calm them down but may not resolve the contributor and when the parent leaves, the child may again express upset by crying.

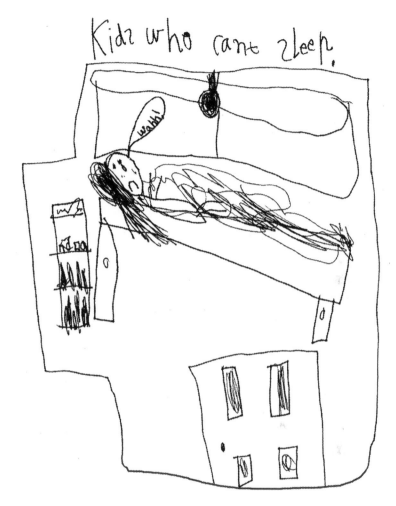

Figure 3.8   Sometimes kids can't fall asleep, even when they want to.

There are so many factors. It is not surprising that numerous books have been written on the topic of children and sleep, and why so many parents are tearing out their hair in relation to their children and sleep!

Action Plan

It helps to be more insightful as to what is going on for your child and to be able to come up with positive solutions if you are in a good energy state yourself. Reducing energy body stress is the first step.

Energy body stress contributes to feeling that you will *never* get any sleep and this child will *never, ever* sleep on its own.

A calm person holding them is settling and soothing for a child, especially for small babies. I recognised this in my daughter, who seemed to hate to sleep when she was a baby! I would hold her in my arms and deliberately concentrate on relaxing myself with deep breathing. She would also relax along with me, her breathing changing and her tension releasing.

Sleep Protocol

1. De-stress until you feel clear, calm and relaxed by tapping for, "relaxed", "peace", "calm", "release stress", or something similar. If this is hard (sleep deprivation makes *everything* harder!), try to tag-team with someone and spend your off time on de-stressing and energising.

2. Notice how you're feeling and concentrate on deep breathing and softening any tension you're holding.

3. Look at your child and ask yourself, "What would help her or him settle down easily for sleep?" Whatever comes up, take positive action on this. For example, my 6-year-old daughter often wants company, a chat, and a hug. If I have followed steps 1 and 2, I can offer her this, unworried about her needing me to come and do this every night even when she is an adult. Children can ask for these things by way of seeming excuses. So, "I want you to read me more stories," might be purely to satisfy the need for company, a chat and a hug, but in words that kids can easily express.

4. Proxy tap on behalf of your child, or, if they are comfortable with it, you can tap on them or with them. I've had good success with my kids by tapping in their company on "happy sleep", "yes to sleep", "ready for sleep", "relax", or simply just "sleep".

A mother's relaxing voice and gentle repetition is also soothing for them. You can find the right words and energy for your child by asking them or tuning in to how they are feeling about sleeping. For example, when I asked my son how he felt about going to sleep, he told me that, "My body says 'no' to sleep". I tapped for, "yes to sleeping", with him as way to help him with that.

5. Instead of tapping the points, gently stroke them or massage them, maybe in conjunction with a song or story or bedtime conversation.

6. One of the most important elements for me relating to sleep and children (aside from de-stressing myself) was letting go of other peoples' rules and expectations of what was right or wrong. Just because it is written in a book or claimed as the holy grail of sleep, doesn't make it right for *you* or your children.

   Does it feel good to have your children co-sleep with you? Does it feel better to have your children sleep in their own rooms? Does your arrangement support all of you and help you to get a healthy amount of sleep? Does it support your whole family or is it chosen because of fear or avoidance?

   If there are approaches that you feel guilty or uncertain about doing, or aren't even sure which approach to take to begin with, by all means use EFT and tap for them! EFT can help you gain clarity by helping you let go of the things that are not truthful for you, and enhancing the things that are. You cannot *tap in* something that is not your truth. So, for example, tapping for things like, "I don't know where my daughter should sleep", "I don't know if I should co-sleep", or "I don't know what the best approach to bedtime is", may give you good insights going forward.

   Your choices for your family are yours alone, and what is best for you and the individuals in your family is not necessarily going to be what works for another family. Making peace with that, accepting your choices, and being proud of the way in which you are supporting your family is *wonderful*! There may be benefits in tapping for affirmations such as, "I am at peace with how my baby sleeps", "I accept my choices relating to my son's bedtime", or "I am proud of our sleep routine". Again, it's possible an element of untruth may pop up during the tapping process, so repeat with several rounds to gain clear insight.

7. Above all else, this really *will* pass. You're doing brilliantly. Your children are learning.

Tantrums and Tears Over "Nothing"

Basic Principles

Kids can be highly emotional at times and it can be frustrating when there are tears and tantrums about things that do not even seem to matter, such as, crying over ice melting, upset about cut apples not being able to be put back together, or tears because they didn't get to switch on the light.

As irrational as they might seem, those tears and tantrums are an important message. They are an indication of an energy system that is upset or stressed. Telling a child to stop being silly, laughing at or making fun of their overreactions, or expecting them to control their feelings so they can get a reward or avoid punishment is not acknowledging the reasons underlying what they are expressing that need attention.

A child's overreactions could be explained by any number of stressors affecting them: feeling hot and uncomfortable on a summer's day, a sibling's birthday when they are not getting as much attention, the challenging transition of starting school, specific things that happened that day that bothered them, or their reaction to the stress their mother feels because she is going through a tough time.

All of these things and more can contribute to energy body stress. The more stress that is felt, the more likely it is that an *irrational* reaction to things may occur. The stress is what needs to be treated and attended to, not the tears.

Figure 3.9   Even if it seems like nothing to you, a child can have very real emotions that make them very sad.

Action Plan

1. I feel that it is important for parents to use compassionate curiosity and allow kids to experience their emotions without taking it personally or as judgement on their parenting abilities. There is a meaningful message within these emotions, even if they are inconvenient or nonsensical. This means no eye-rolling, sighing, teasing, or "Enough!"

   If you are personally troubled by someone else expressing an emotion, chances are that there is some personal difficulty you have in dealing with emotions. If this is so, on your own time, tap several rounds of EFT to de-stress yourself, using such words as, "calm" or "release stress", and then tap on what it is that is annoying you about tantrums or tears in words that resonate with you, such as "demanding", "selfishness", "being a sook", or "misery-guts". Follow where the energy goes in this tapping. If the tapping brings up a memory of your own tantrums or having someone judge you for having emotions, it is well worth pursuing with further EFT rounds. Seeking out an EFT practitioner is good support.

You may also feel your child's behaviour is a reflection on you as a parent. This should also be focused on with tapping. Your setup could be something like, "How does it make me feel when my child has a tantrum in public?"

Once you know that crying and tantrums are expressions of a person's energy state, it takes the fear out of those emotions being expressed and helps to gain clarity you can use to support the child and give attention to how they feel, but not necessarily aim to take away their problems.

2.   Be present with the child and give loving attention, reassurance and openness. Send them an intention of something like, "I see you, I hear you, I feel you, and I'm here". Refer to the How to De-Stress a Child section in part 2 on page 38. Follow your intuition and apply any actions that you can to support them.

3.   Save conversations about specifics for a later time when they have calmed down and if they are still bothered by it. If your child is not open to talking about it, you can proxy tap for them. A plain and simple setup could be, "Melanie's upset".

Toilet Training

Basic Principles

Toilet training is a major source of stress for a parent. It seems at the time that there will never be an end to puddles of urine everywhere or soiled poo-pants! But the inevitable end does come, when things just seem to click and the nightmare is over for the parent.

First things first, toilet training needs to go by awareness, interest, and experience. I don't believe that you can make a child toilet train before they are ready, and it is likely to be stressful for everyone if attempts are made prematurely.

In relation to poo, a body that is relaxed and calm allows physiological systems do what is needed. It is when energy body stress increases

Figure 3.10   While toilets make sense to adults, they can be big and scary to some children. A big open hole, who knows what the lid might do!

(such as when a person is fearful) that problems start. That stress can contribute to outward actions of closing up, tightening, or stopping. In terms of going to the toilet, this might cause constipation, avoidance, accidents in pants, or tantrums.

Action Plan

The most important factor to keep on top of in toilet training is your own stress. The thoughts of, "I am going to be washing poopy pants forever!" or "She will *never* sit on the toilet to wee!" are all stress-driven! Parents know on some level that a healthy child *will* learn to use the toilet, but the stress of the experience is clouding that knowledge.

So whenever those thoughts or feelings bubble up, your focus should be to reduce your energy body stress. Doing so will also allow you to be more intuitive so you can tune into your child and know whether this is the right time for them or not, without that stress clouding your connection to them and what they are needing. You can always choose to pause the process until it feels right for you and your child.

Accidents are frustrating and extra cause of workload. This experience is exacerbated by energy body stress when you feel that you are never, ever going to get on top of all the laundry because of the endless washing of sheets and clothes. That feels true, but it's not (trust me), and de-stressing is key.

When my children were having difficulties learning how to poo on the toilet, I created a Poo Protocol! It was effective with two children at times of constipation or just plain tension relating to pooping.

Prerequisites for using the poo protocol:

- Child having difficulty pooing.
- Parent keen to help.

Poo Protocol

1. Parent is calm (if not, then de-stress).
2. Parent is giving the child their attention with eye contact.
3. Parent taps for "I relax and let go", saying it out loud, and concentrating on breathing well and deeply. Tap on the child if they allow it and like it, otherwise tap on yourself on their behalf.
4. Parent encourages child with a smile and praise.
5. Wait for the inevitable plop and splash.

Other supportive options are:

- De-stressing yourself with, "calm", "peace", "relax", etc. Yes I've mentioned this before, but I can't stress it enough!
- Tapping for "Johnny using the toilet" by way of proxy tapping for the child. You could also get specific, such as "Johnny's fear of using the toilet".
- Tapping for any qualities of the toilet that might be fearful to a small person such as the noise of the water, the fear of falling

in, the fear of being flushed away, or not understanding what is happening.

- Aside from tapping, I've also drawn pictures to demonstrate to my kids how poo is made and also about how a toilet works. Information like that can be calming to them if fears come from not understanding what is happening. I've demonstrated the process with toys using toy toilets and wiping their bottoms afterward; my kids felt fine about it. Role-playing through play with toys (if suited to your child) can be a light way for kids to express their fears, such as "Teddy is scared to poo. Oh, it's okay Teddy, pooing won't hurt you!"

Transitions or Changes Causing Upset

Basic Principles

A change in an activity or location can be a source of stress. I've read that the greatest sources of stress for an adult are moving to a new house, getting a new job, and losing a job. All potentially big changes.

When we are in a certain place doing a certain activity, it is known and understood. The familiarity is comforting. Make a change and we might feel stress and react with an increase of energy body stress symptoms. In children this can include crying, irritation, shutting down, non-compliance, or not listening.

Change and transition can also be a source of stress on a number of levels if someone is removed from a situation they are heartily enjoying.

If someone is in a calm and happy state, they may be more able to make transitions without much upheaval, but if someone is already a little stressed, a change can result in that stress being intensified and this can show up in *irrational* reactions to what feels like a simple task. ("Huh?" says the confused parent, "I just want you to have a bath...! It's not *that* bad.")

We don't have to avoid transitions, but we can recognise that they may be a source of stress. Any difficulty that shows up in a child undergoing a transition is for a valid reason and worthy of attention and support.

Figure 3.11   It's not easy to stop doing something you enjoy just because somebody else wants you to.

Action Plan

1. Be aware of the child's current state. Are they already stressed or irritated and showing this with behaviour that is closed down, agitated or restless? Are they deeply immersed in an activity they love that it would be a source of stress for them to leave?

    Use that information in relation to your transition. Offer your child attention, water, food, gentle touch, encouragement, or praise. Talk or play with them or alongside them. Sometimes you don't have the luxury of time to do this, but being respectful of what they are doing can help to shorten how long a task takes to do. You wouldn't be happy if you had to get up from a warm and comfy bed to deal with something in the front yard or to have your favourite TV show cut short by the TV being turned off.

If you are aware of your child's current state, you will be better able to connect and recognise their joy, relaxation or pleasure. It will then be a natural extension for the child to respectfully approach a transition with you.

2. Children are very much pleasure seekers, as are nearly all of us, so they may be more enticed to do something if it is clear to them what benefits they get out of it. Adults become used to doing stuff they hate. There's plenty of time for children to learn that not everything will have an enjoyable benefit. There's no need to teach your babies how restrictive life can be. Childhood is for fun, adventure, and learning and discovering through play!

    Transition, done in ways that are respectful and supportive, recognises the child's interests and motivations and what they love. For example, when it comes to bath time, here are some suggestions on how to handle the transition:

    - "After this episode is finished it's time for a bath."

    - "Maybe your toy cars could join you in the bath tub! Can we race them there together?"

    - "Would Barbie like a swim in the bath at her luxury hotel?"

    - "I'd like to run a bath soon, would you like to play with bubbles or bath paints today?"

    - "What cool PJs would you like to put on after you've had your bath tonight?"

    - "I know you're enjoying that game, but it's nearly bath time. How about if you play for another 10 or 15 minutes and then stop to take a bath."

- "I like to play Snap too. When you've had a bath we could play Snap together!"

3. If the idea of getting your children to transition to a task becomes a source of dread and stress, attend to it with several rounds of EFT! Your sense of dread might come across in your words and attitude and the transition is off on the wrong foot before you even begin. We are lucky to have a tool to *clear* the way so we can truly start with a *clear* slate instead of holding onto something indefinitely. Use simple setups like, "bath time", "having to get them off the iPad", "bedtime", "happy bedtime", or "easy bedtime".

   When dealing with nightly transitions, it's important to feel clear, bright, enthusiastic and ready, not holding onto the weight of day's many difficulties. Chances are if your kids are not used to making a stress-free transition, they will go into the usual mode of refusal to the things they dislike. Do not let that put you off! Persist in focusing on *you* feeling good about it, even if they are not there yet.

4. Also observe how *you* feel about the particular areas that your children find difficult. I noticed that the things I said to my daughter about her "dawdling to bed" and "taking forever to go to sleep because you keep doing every other thing instead", I could easily be saying to myself!

   A good—but maybe challenging—question for both parents to ask themselves might be: "What is it about this difficulty that reminds me of myself?" Notice any sensations or emotions in yourself that show up, because they may not be *on the radar*. If your children say, "I hate going to bed", ask yourself how *you* feel about it and use that as your setup for rounds of EFT. Check in between each round of tapping to see how you are feeling afterward. Keep using how you feel about it as a setup until you feel neutral, and then tap for how you *want* to feel about it, such as "easy bedtime", or "I love showers".

Part Four

In Conclusion

It excites and delights me to share this information from my heart to yours. I know that some of this approach is very different from what you might have learned in the past in other parenting books or the instruction you may have received from others, such as your parents, but I have seen the benefits of this approach in my own home and know what gifts it offers.

It feels good to know that I can be an effective parent without threats, ignoring my child, sending them away or punishing them. Those things never sat right with me yet I did not know what else to do. By using EFT, I was excited to see my children and my role as a parent through *eyes of energy*. EFT has helped to make me aware of how improving energy movement and reducing or eliminating energy body stress and blockages can help me every day.

I know with certainty that the reliable structural approach of this modern energy work can only help family harmony. I am very much looking forward to a gradual shift in how we parent and care for children as well as how we care for ourselves. We all deserve compassion and understanding at various times in our lives when we behave badly because of energy body stress levels or other circumstances which made it difficult to be a happy or kind person. We, as well as our children, are doing the best we can with the circumstances we are undergoing as well as the experiences we have been through. We deserve forgiveness, love, and attention, not harsh criticism and avoidance.

I wish for all children to be seen not as problems to be fixed, but as small humans that are showing us in the best way that they can what they are going through on the inside. I wish for adults to respectfully acknowledge and accept that, for whatever reason, at times children have challenges and bad days, the same as any adult.

I wish for us to respect the fact that we as adults have had a much longer time on the planet to understand what things are and how things work. A child, with their limited experience, may find these situation difficult to absorb and adjust to.

I wish for us to be more patient with these little people, who are actually kind-hearted, loving, and wonderful people, even if they're having a hard time at the moment.

I wish for the role of parenting not to be expected as something that moulds or shapes a child into how the parent wants them to be, but for the parent to see children as they truly are and allow their personality to show confidently.

I wish for a new approach to be taken to *naughty* children. An approach that is compassionate and supports the child's energy body, particularly when it comes to the role of energy body stress.

I wish for emotional expressions to be seen without fear and as a message that is not a personal insult to ourselves as parents nor our abilities, but a simple honest message. I wish for emotions to not carry with them a stigma of difficulty. In childhood and beyond.

I wish for each of us the freedom to acknowledge (and have others acknowledge) that how we feel is 100% valid for each of us in relation to what we are going through, now or in the past.

I wish for an increase in loving-hearted, calm and happy people available to give pure attention to a child when it shows that it is struggling.

Most of all, I wish for all parents to recognise that they themselves are unique with unique children who are going through their own unique experiences. We have to come at this journey free of expectations about how the experience will be for us and also free of expectations of how our child's experience will be.

I want us to ban *should* from our vocabularies when it comes to our child and also ourselves. When you find yourself saying, "He should behave better than that", remember that he's a *child* with limited coping mechanisms and he's behaving that way because he is stressed out. So let's work with that instead of resisting it and branding it as unacceptable.

Have you ever said to yourself, "I should be a better parent and shout less. Because I shout I must be a bad parent"? Instead of branding yourself like that, take an approach of curiosity and look to reduce the stressors that led to that yelling being a common occurrence. As parents, when we reduce our own energy body stress, we become clearer and more creative with our solutions and approaches. Refusing, denying and ignoring are all approaches that are stagnant in terms of energy. Acceptance, openness, exploration are all energetic movements and lead us to the potential for change.

Children who are unafraid to express themselves truthfully and have their feelings and difficulties accepted, are more likely to feel confident and secure in themselves and become adults that reach out unashamedly when they are going through a tough time.

So let's start today and work step by step, bit by bit, towards being calm and de-stressed enough to be present with our children, whatever it is that they are going through.

Teach them they are worthy of respect and receiving what they need. Show them by our own actions how people should treat each other.

Demonstrate how emotions aren't something to hide away from, by working to be in a state where we can receive whatever emotions they are presenting to us.

Let's be clear and objective enough so that we can see how the behaviour, emotions and actions are a symptom of something greater going on. They are a clue for where we need to focus not a symptom that we need to squash down or train them out of.

Let's see our children not as little people to mould and gain compliance from, but family members, team members, and intelligent little people with passions, dreams, ideas and inspirations, who can work with us for the betterment of the entire family. Let's set a tone of allowing and accepting them, unconditionally.

As good and strong leaders of our family, we have the opportunity to be our child's first teacher and to show them what compassion looks like, what connectedness and unconditional support looks like, what it looks like to be aware of other human beings.

The flow-on effects of a child raised with that outlook and awareness are unknown, yet have great potential for the world as we know it.

Let's be unapologetically human enough to admit when we've made a mistake or made a wrong choice because of where we were at the time. Let's teach our children, in the act of parenting, how it's all about trying our best with the resources that we have, and that we can try out new approaches and ideas to see what happens.

Let's also celebrate our successes and pat our backs with the things that we are doing right and well, seeing life not as a test to pass or fail, but an experience to be enjoyed as an adventure, with ourselves as cheerleaders and not drill sergeants.

Ultimately, all parents are doing the best that they can depending on their experiences and challenges. I acknowledge all of us for giving love to our children in the best capacity that we can muster at any given moment.

With love and courage,
Kelly Burch
February 2014

References

Original EFT by Gary Craig. Developed from TFT by Dr Roger Callahan.

Heart & Soul Protocol, 2010, by Silvia Hartmann. Developed from *Classic EFT Protocol* by Gary Craig.

Heart Healing, 2003, by Silvia Hartmann. EmoTrance, Level 2.

SUE Scale, 2009, by Silvia Hartmann, Events Psychology.

Energy Body Stress, 2011, by Silvia Hartmann. Developed from *EmoTrance—Energy Nutrition*, 2002.

Explaining Energy to Teens, by Kelly Burch. http://theamt.com/explaining_energy_to_teens.htm.

The Aspects Model of Identity Through Time, developed from Project Sanctuary by Silvia Hartmann, 1993/2006.

Emotions Definition—EmoTrance, 2002, Silvia Hartmann.

The Sixth Sense—EmoTrance, 2011, Silvia Hartmann.

Energetic Relationships, 2002, Silvia Hartmann.

Group Entity, 2011, Silvia Hartmann.

Intuition—EmoTrance, 2011, by Silvia Hartmann.

Love Energy, 1993, based on The Harmony Program by Silvia Hartmann.

About the Author

Kelly Burch is an energist who is passionate about using energy techniques to explore life and to make a difference in areas that feel stuck or unworkable.

She is enjoying exploring parenthood with the support of energy and learning more about her two children, herself, and life in the process.

She has also explored the topic of autism in her project during which she donated energy techniques support to autistic families in order to learn more about the role of energy in autism.

Additional Reading

BIG Ted's Guide to Tapping
Alex Kent, Illustrated by Jen Smith
Turn Negative Emotions Into Positive Ones with BIG Ted

Join the loveable BIG Ted as he guides you and your child through the near miraculous Emotional Freedom Techniques (EFT). You'll both discover how your emotions are transformed by tapping with your magic finger on points around your face, body and hands.

BIG Ted is suitable for children of all ages and adults will also benefit from joining in with the fun.

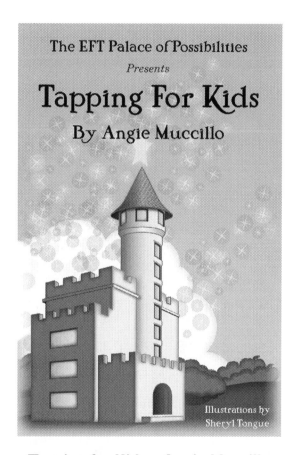

The EFT Palace of Possibilities

Presents

Tapping For Kids

By Angie Muccillo

Illustrations by
Sheryl Tongue

Tapping for Kids—Angie Muccillo
The exciting book aimed at teaching children EFT!

Tapping For Kids is designed to help children overcome traumas and problems of everyday life by using EFT. Through a mix of story, activities and rhymes the book enhances children's learning and shows them how EFT can be used to help them overcome their fears, worries and everyday traumas, while at the same time building up their self-esteem.

The story in the book is set within "The EFT Palace of Possibilities for Kids", a multilevel healing high rise where its 'Caretaker', known as the TapMeister, runs play shops to help children 'master the art of tapping'—a popular new kids movement taking the world by storm!

The book is filled with illustrations demonstrating how to use the points and numerous exercises to make using EFT fun for kids.

Tapping For Kids is a perfect gift for any children in your life!

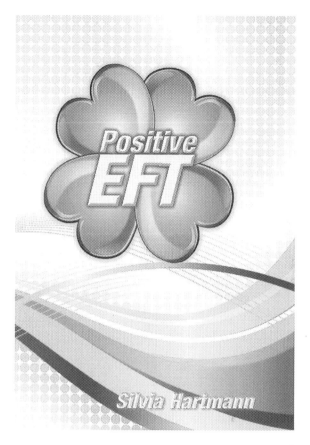

Positive EFT—Silvia Hartmann
Stronger, Faster, Smarter but Most of All, Happier

Positive EFT is the antidote to depression, anxiety, stress, temper tantrums, low energy, misery, impatience, indecision, confusion and feeling helpless, hopeless, powerless and alone. Positive EFT makes introducing EFT an easy, enjoyable, uplifting experience. Perfect for self help and an absolute "must have!" for the modern practitioner.

Digging around endlessly in the traumas of your past is not the answer to a happy life NOW. By bringing POSITIVE energies into your energy body, you completely transform the way you feel.

Quick and easy-to-use, Positive EFT is an ENORMOUSLY POWERFUL addition to your healing practice. Positive EFT is what the world needs, right now.

Energy EFT—Silvia Hartmann
Next Generation Tapping & Emotional Freedom Techniques

Silvia Hartmann, chair of The AMT, takes Gary Craig's classic EFT to the next level with this comprehensive book that is an absolute must-buy for anyone interested in energy and its use in turning negative emotions into positive ones. All emotions can be worked with, including Stress, Anxiety, Fear & PTSD. Energy EFT is suitable for both beginners, energy workers in different modalities and also top-level EFT master practitioners & trainers wanting to know more.

Using EFT with energy in mind, you can now experience faster, more focused, more logical EFT self-help treatments and go much further into the realms of empowerment, mental clarity and having all the energy you need to succeed in life.

The EFT Master Practitioner Distance Learning Course
Silvia Hartmann & Kelly Burch
Includes Full Tutor Support, Certification & 12-DVD Set

The new AMT EFT Master Practitioner course is the first major update on the theory and practice of EFT Emotional Freedom Techniques since 1999. The AMT EFT Master Practitioner Course takes recent worldwide developments of EFT and brings them together so that the student can experience a clear, logical, direct and powerful way to resolve problems with EFT Emotional Freedom Techniques.

Since the time when EFT Emotional Freedom Techniques was first introduced, much has been learned about the cause-and-effect relationships between energy, emotions and how people think, feel and do. Indeed, it was the practice of EFT which led the way to many new discoveries about the basic principles of "how people work."

The successful student will gain the AMT EFT Master Practitioner Certification and become a full member of The Association for Meridan & Energy Therapies (The AMT).

The Golden Horse
Original Fairy Tales by Silvia Hartmann

Fairy tales especially, with their timeless settings, their powerful imagery and rhythms, their patterns and their unfoldments, shape our lives and thinking more than most will ever know.

The Golden Horse is the perfect antidote for negative "lessons" taught in traditional fairy tales with powerful stories of true magic, of power, indeed, of our personal, god-given power to change the world and live lives filled with enchantment.*

Perfect for sharing with children or the child within, perfect and unusual tools for self help and therapy, these stories can be used to change minds, and hearts, and most of all, re-connect us to the magic we once knew was real when we were still a child.